MORGAN
FREEMAN

MORGAN FREEMAN

A BIOGRAPHY

Kathleen Tracy

Published by Barricade Books Inc.
185 Bridge Plaza North
Suite 308-A
Fort Lee, NJ 07024
www.barricadebooks.com

Library of Congress Cataloging-in-Publication Data
A copy of this title's Library of Congress Cataloging-in-Publication Data
is available on request from the Library of Congress.

ISBN 1-56980-307-2

First Printing
Manufactured in the United States of America

Contents

A Look Back;
a Glimpse Forward

FOR MANY MOVIE buffs and historians, 1939 remains Hollywood's greatest creative year, boasting an almost breathless number of films destined to become celluloid classics: *The Wizard of Oz, Goodbye, Mr. Chips, Of Mice and Men, The Young Mr. Lincoln, Destry Rides Again, Stagecoach, Mr. Smith Goes to Washington, Wuthering Heights, Juarez, Dark Victory, Ninotchka.*

None, however, would have the legacy of *Gone with the Wind*—both in and out of darkened movie theaters. The melodramatic adaptation of Margaret Mitchell's Pulitzer Prize–winning novel set in the American South during the Civil War and Reconstruction became an iconic standard of film industry success.

The movie also became the unwitting mirror of race relations in pre–World War II America and shone an unwelcome spotlight on how Hollywood treated its own when black cast members were summarily prevented from participating in the film's premiere.

It's sobering to realize that Hattie McDaniel, who played Mammy, was a first-generation freeman. Her father had been born into slavery on a Virginia plantation, and it speaks to the unique flexibility of American society that a mere generation later his daughter was a working actress. However, the welcome mat was extended only so far.

McDaniel spent most of her career playing maids because those were the only roles available for the majority of black actresses. Her oft-repeated quote—"Why should I complain about making $7,000 a week playing a maid? If I didn't, I'd be making $7 a week being one"—was at once gracious and pointed.

Despite being a well-known performer—she appeared in ninety-five films—McDaniel had no illusions. When *Gone with the Wind* premiered in Atlanta, she was conspicuously absent. To save her producer from being put in the position of having to defend her attendance, Hattie begged off by claiming illness. But the stark reality was, because of Georgia's segregation laws, McDaniel and the other African-American cast members would have endured the humiliation of facing state-sanctioned racism.

While McDaniel would have been allowed to appear on stage at the Grand Theater alongside the white actors, she would have been prohibited from attending the whites-only Junior League Ball or sitting in the theater auditorium with her costars to watch the film. There would not have even been a bathroom—or front entrance—in the building for her use.

Perhaps the most insulting slight was when her picture was removed from the back cover of the premiere's souvenir program so as not to upset Atlanta's white society mavens attending the movie. Leonard Leff reported in *The Atlantic* that frustrated producer David O. Selznick complained the incident put him "on the spot of seeming ungrateful for what I honestly feel is one of the great supporting performances of all times."

Although Selznick felt obliged to play the politics of the time, Clark Gable did not, and he threatened to boycott the premiere if McDaniel was not guaranteed a welcome. But his stance and the publicity it generated did little to change many hearts and minds. Knowing he was waging a losing battle, McDaniel convinced Gable to attend, averting a publicity nightmare for Selznick.

It wasn't the last time McDaniel would find herself on the racial front lines. Just months after the Atlanta snub, she became the first black actress nominated for an Oscar and the first African-American to attend the Academy Awards as a guest. Although many African-Americans criticized McDaniel for having made a career out of playing domestics, others saw it as a turning point. Leff reports that Selznick received a letter from a national black sorority hailing her nomination with naïve optimism.

"We trust that discrimination and prejudice will be wiped away in the selection of the winner of this award, for without Miss McDaniel, there would be no *Gone with the Wind*."

As expected, on January 29, 1940, McDaniel made history by winning the Oscar; she read an acceptance speech that had been prepared by a studio writer.

Academy of Motion Picture Arts and Sciences, fellow members of the motion picture industry and honored guests: This is one of the happiest moments of my life, and I want to thank each one of you who had a part in selecting for one of the awards, for your kindness. It has made me feel very, very humble; and I shall always hold it as a beacon for anything that I may be able to do in the future. I sincerely hope I shall always be a credit to my race and to the motion picture industry. My heart is too full to tell you just how I feel, and may I say thank you and God bless you.

Contemporaries who hoped McDaniel's recognition would immediately open doors for minority actors were bitterly disappointed as progress remained glacially slow. The Oscars in particular remained diversity challenged into the next millennium, prompting Chris Rock to famously comment during one Oscar telecast, "Look at this crowd. . . . It's like the Million *White* Man March here today."

While such barbs may be justified, the landscape *is* changing and over the last half century new generations of African-American actors are enjoying unprecedented success and accolades only made possible by the pioneering efforts of such performers as McDaniel.

Perhaps nobody represents this evolution better than Morgan Freeman.

Although he was only a toddler when McDaniel broke the Oscar color barrier, Freeman's career shares a certain kinship with hers, insofar as while others may seek change through activism and protest, Freeman, like McDaniel before him, has instigated change from within through his work, longevity, and presence.

With a body of work that spans five decades, Freeman has risen through the Hollywood pecking order against the backdrop of America's cultural revolution and its conservative aftermath, in many ways reflecting the growing pains of a society—and entertainment industry—still struggling to make racial equality a reality.

Typically, Freeman chooses to see the positives. Backstage at the 2005 Oscars, when asked the importance of two African-American men—he for the supporting role in *Million Dollar Baby* and Jamie Foxx's Best Actor Oscar for *Ray*—sweeping the acting awards for the first time, he observed, "Hollywood is continuing to make history. Life goes on. Things change. Nothing stays the same. We are evolving."

So is Freeman, and through it all, he manages to transcend race, age, and creed and now finds himself a reluctant American treasure. Dignified and wry, humble yet confident, he's the journeyman actor who suddenly found himself an overnight success at an age when many actors, especially those of color, are forced into retirement for lack of work.

He has quietly carved out a place in the film history as one of the most accomplished actors—of any color—to ever charm the big screen. And yet he remains an enigma. His aversion to the limelight is as powerful as his passion for acting, so few are aware that his off-screen life has been as dramatic as many of his on-screen exploits. From his childhood in the depression-era south to years as a literally starving artist working regional theater to Hollywood's belated embrace, Freeman's often hard-scrabble existence is what now informs his work with his signature grace and world-weary wisdom.

If Hattie McDaniel became film's enduring symbol of racism, then Morgan Freeman represents Hollywood's greatest salvation by reminding audiences that talent and style is truly color-blind.

I T'S OFTEN SAID that to understand who somebody has become, it's necessary to go back and see where they began. That adage seems to be particularly relevant when talking about anyone born and raised in the American south. More than a geographic location, the South is a way of life, borne of and informed by its unique history, much of it steeped in myth and mythology.

Twentieth-century writers and poets tapped into the symbolism of the dying Old South as the basis for the Southern Gothic genre, using a strong sense of place to evoke almost visceral images that reeked of the passions and emotions of a south that no longer truly existed except in the hearts of its progeny.

Tennessee Williams once commented that "in the South there's a greater sense of honor, of decency. . . . I don't think of my people as damned—not as long as they keep courage and gallantry. Those are important and very Southern qualities, bred in the bones of the people I wrote about, such as Amanda Wingfield" (*The Glass Menagerie*).

But there has always been a more complex, darker side of the South, where modern lynchings and the birth of the Civil Rights Movement coincided and where blacks felt more comfortable despite the overt prejudice because they found the bias in the north more subversive, therefore, more dishonest and dangerous. At least in the South, you knew your enemy and could adjust accordingly.

Morgan Freeman, for one, believes that's why it's too easy an out to blame racism for not achieving success. While some doors may be closed, there are others always waiting to be walked through.

"I don't care what you do. Whatever obstacles you run into, it's easy to say, *You know, they wouldn't let me. I wanted to, I tried, but I'm black so.* . . . It's the easiest cop-out. So, it's a little more difficult . . . so what? Who's got it easy? And I think that racism is not a one-way street. If I constantly tell you that you're against me, pretty soon you're going to say I don't want to get near this guy."

Freeman also takes exception to the importance placed on racial labels, such as African-American. "I'm not an African," he says coolly.

There are African-Americans here—they're from Ghana and Nigeria, Senegal, Cameroon, Sierra Leone. They can name the country that they're from. A lot of them are first-generation African-Americans.

If you want to give *me* an adjective, call me black. That's a Diaspora. But don't call me African. I'm an American; long, long bloody history, just like every other American. When I was a kid, we were "colored." Then we became "Negro." Then we became Afro, in the sixties, Afro-American . . . so this quest for identity— it's like, No. 1, misguided.

All of which is not to say the American experience for the southern black community hasn't endured some unique challenges and obstacles.

In the years following the Civil War, most blacks chose to stay in the South and for a while enjoyed a heady sense of newfound freedom. Although the races tended not to mix socially, blacks and whites lived side by side, equally protected under Reconstruction laws. Educators from the North flooded to the South to teach former slaves how to read and write, and cities began to swell with an influx of rural blacks who moved to urban areas in search of better wages and housing.

In short order, it was more than the white majority could stand. Given a huge assist by the Supreme Court, many southern states and municipalities began passing laws aimed at eroding the protections granted under Reconstruction. The first blow was when the high court voided the Civil Rights Act as unconstitutional. That led to a flurry of anti-African-American segregation legislation that became collectively known as the Jim Crow laws, named after a minstrel song about blacks.

By the dawn of the twentieth century, African-Americans were tightly controlled by state sanctioned—and government approved—segregation. Although the court ruled facilities needed to be "separate but equal," the reality was Jim Crow relegated most blacks to poverty and second-class citizenry. Admittance to schools, hospitals, restaurants, and even public parks was limited to designated areas. In several states, it was illegal for an African-American to marry a white, and some cities imposed special curfews for black citizens.

Oddly, though, these blatant social injustices weren't enough to force most blacks from their communities. They simply adapted until nature and the resulting economic hardships forced them out.

Starting in 1913, the southern cotton crops were pummeled by a series of devastating calamities. First, the global price of cotton fell, forcing some farmers—and their sharecroppers—out of business. Then an infestation of a new lethal vermin—boll weevils—decimated crops.

It's believed weevils first invaded America in 1892 via Brownsville, Texas. Thirty years later the weevil had spread throughout all the eastern cotton growing states, from Mississippi to Virginia, at a rate of fifty-five miles a year. The speed with which the weevil spread caught many off guard and buckled local economies. That, plus the severe floods of 1915 in the Mississippi Valley, prompted the start of what became known as the Great Migration, one of the largest relocations of citizens in U.S. history, which literally changed the face of urban America. Between 1915 and 1930 it is estimated more than 2 million blacks moved up the Mississippi and via railways to northern industrial cities.

Despite the change of location, prejudice still ran rampant, with southern blacks often turned away by factory owners unwilling to hire people of color. But that changed with World War I. Now in desperate need of workers, employers in cities such as Chicago welcomed black workers. Likewise, black women found steady work as maids.

Of all cities, Chicago became a prime destination for southern blacks—one reason for the explosion of blues clubs. The Windy City also boasted the most influential black-run paper in the country, the *Chicago Defender*. By the time Morgan Freeman was born on June 1, 1937, Chicago had one of the largest and politically active black communities in the country.

Freeman's toddler years were spent in his birth town of Memphis, Tennessee. Raising six kids necessitated two incomes, and when Morgan was born, his parents were both working in a local hospital. Hoping to find better wages, the elder Freemans joined the exodus and relocated to Chicago. Rather than try to establish themselves while caring for their large brood, Morgan, one of the younger children, was sent to live with his paternal grandmother in Charleston, Mississippi.

His earliest memories are of hot, humid summer days. "Running. Dust. Sweat," Freeman recalled, conjuring images with lyrical allusion.

"I walked out the door, there was cotton"—the fields where his ancestors worked as slaves. "I can remember playing in the yard at my Big Mama's house. Big Mama was my grandmother's sister, and she had this big old house in the country. I used to go out and make little towns. I'd scratch out roads with a stick, you know, and then drive my toy cars on them. When you're a child and get real close to those miniatures, they can look really real.

"One of my uncles had either a Ford or a Chevrolet, I can't remember which. Then the war started in '41, and two of my uncles were called away."

His dad also enlisted but was soon discharged. "He was not war material," Freeman recalled with a short laugh.

During the school year, Morgan was raised by his grandmother. In the summer, he would go stay in Chicago with his parents, who had found good paying jobs. His dad worked in the stockyards, and his mom played piano in a church. They lived in Chicago's South Side, a black enclave that became known as Bronzeville by the residents.

When he was six years old, Freeman suffered the first major loss of his life. His beloved grandmother died. Not only did he lose his emotional touchstone, but he also lost his childhood home.

"Up until my grandmother's death, all I remember is fun," Freeman recalls. "I would have stayed there indefinitely had she not died."

It was one thing to visit Chicago for several weeks during the summer school break, quite another to live there year round, especially during a typically frigid winter with the wind whipping off Lake Michigan like frozen razor blades. "The cold hit me right in the face," he admits.

It wasn't just the weather that provided a shock to the youngster's system. Instead of cotton fields dotting the countryside, Morgan found himself wandering gritty, cramped neighborhoods that were as airlessly stifling in the summer as they were brittle with cold during the winter. Where Mississippi offered open spaces, still nights, and star-freckled skies, Chicago was a noisy, cramped concrete forest with towering buildings that blocked breeze and sunlight alike. The sheer number of people living within city limits reduced personal space to little more than elbow room, particularly in the crowded poorer neighborhoods such as Bronzeville.

"The South Side was just chock-a-block with black people living in small apartments that had indoor plumbing," Freeman recalls. "There was no great exposure to another world. I was in the fourth grade when I saw a white teacher for the first time."

Unlike European immigrants such as the Italians or the Irish who were able to assimilate throughout the city, blacks were stuck in the South Side under the ongoing social apartheid of the day. Inevitably different factions within the community established turfs, a forerunner to the gangs that would brutalize Chicago in the 1960s and later. Many kids, like Freeman, were given the Sophie's Choice of either trying to fit in and become associated with a gang or risk veering clear, thereby setting themselves up as potential targets.

"Living on the South Side for me was an untenable situation," Morgan recalled years later.

It was a jungle. You had to belong to some kind of gang just to survive; you couldn't be a loner. And we were all budding street hoodlums, because to be in a gang you had to do something criminal. I stole; I conned; I passed the tests. I didn't like it but I was scared. I'm not the violent type.

It was about turf. And I was just not cut out to be a gangster or to lead a violent life where you're ready to go to the mat with somebody all the time just because they were on the wrong side of the street or whatever. I was personally happy with books. I didn't want to fight.

In a case of preferring the devil you know, Freeman ached for the familiar surroundings of Mississippi, Jim Crow be damned.

"Being second class didn't feel wrong or different to me when I was very young. It can't bother you if that's the way life is," he explains. "If you were raised up in Africa and you ate worms it wouldn't bother you, would it? Same thing.

"I grew up in a segregated society that was purposely, obviously, openly segregated," such as the local movie house where he had to sit in the balcony because the ground floor was for whites only.

I wasn't thinking about rising up and going to the Paramount and demanding to be led into the ground floor. I just wanted to go to the movies. I wasn't given any BS about anything else and I went up to the north and you see it and it's insidious. You want to think you're freer, but you're not.

We didn't feel poor in the South, even through we were, but we did in Chicago. We felt destitute. In the south, we felt safer—and I still do.

There is a connection there that people from the South always find. Now it's even more so, considering everything that's happened historically.

To his relief, Freeman's stay in Chicago would prove short-lived. His parents' marriage broke up. Although Freeman seldom discusses his childhood, one factor in the split may be deduced from his father dying at age forty-seven from alcohol-induced cirrhosis. His mother, Mayme Edna, took Morgan back to Mississippi, eventually settling in Greenwood's Baptist Town neighborhood once she remarried Grafton "Son" Curtis. It was there that Freeman enjoyed his first taste of applause, all because of unrequited puppy love.

"There was this doll-like girl I was just crazy about," Freeman explains. "To get her attention, I pulled a chair out from under her. The teacher marched me down the hall, and I figured I was going to the principal's office to get beaten half to death."

But the teacher showed prescience by figuring it was better to channel that youthful exuberance into something constructive rather than bruise it. She took Morgan to another teacher who needed performers for a school play. Freeman was cast as Little Boy Blue.

"I was put on the stage in a little pageant. It was one of the most gratifying things I'd ever done," he remembers. "Doing that little show, I realized that pretending was something I could also do in front of people. Not just under a tree or behind the house or down by the creek."

When he was twelve Freeman participated in—and won—a statewide performing competition, acting in a one-act play.

I played an eleven- or twelve-year-old kid who idolized an older brother just home from the war. . . . We won the district. Then we won the state. I was named best actor. So I was a big man on campus in junior high. I was as much a star in acting as a football player was or a basketball player was. I had a paper route. One time I was going around doing my collections. I signed my name on one of my little receipts, and the customer said, "*Oh, you're Morgan Freeman.*" I just felt famous. At home, I wasn't dramatic at all. I was funny. You know, humor was what you go for to get attention.

I still have the little pin that says, *Best Actor, 1950.*

It wasn't just the applause that appealed to Freeman, it was the process. "It was all of it, from day one of rehearsal to closing night."

After that, "as a teenager, I began to settle into school because I'd discovered extracurricular activities that interested me: music and theater. I became what I suppose you would call a rather serious student. I functioned on attention, I think, and I was getting a lot of attention in school."

Certainly he was getting a lot of recognition—the caption under his senior yearbook photos was *The Actor.*

"When a teacher tells you that you're going to make it, that you've got what it takes, all you can do is keep going. That's a lot of fuel when you're eighteen years old and a world beater, because when your teachers are constantly telling you that you're really something, then you feel like something."

Performing not only gave Freeman confidence, but it also revealed other untapped talents. "I had two left feet for sports but not for dancing. We didn't hang out at McDonald's like some kids today. On Fridays, I went to this little place called the Stand. It had a Wurlitzer that played all the best blues guys—Gatemouth Brown, Lightnin' Hopkins. We'd take over the back room and dance. To this day, I get energized by the blues; even if I'm tired, it's like something else is pushing me onto the dance floor."

One of his other favorite pastimes was watching movies. "When I was a kid, it cost 12 cents to go to the movies. If you could find a milk bottle, you could sell it for a nickel. Soda and beer bottles were worth 2 cents. If you were diligent, you could come up with movie money every day.

"My heroes were Gary Cooper, Spencer Tracy. Of course, by the time I graduated from high school, there was Sidney Poitier, picking all the roles that I wanted."

He was partial to war films, with their black-and-white notions of patriotic heroism that downplayed the messy horrors of combat. "I also wanted to fly, I wanted to have wings. I was a child of the war propaganda films, and I had a lot of fantasies."

So despite his enthusiasm for acting, after Freeman graduated from Greenwood High School, he turned down a theater scholarship to Jackson State University—"I didn't think a drama scholarship in Mississippi was going to get me very far"—to enlist in the Air Force. "My aim in life when I graduated from high school was to get out of Mississippi."

Although as a child Freeman had taken the oppression of southern racial bigotry in stride, the implication of segregation eventually sank in and rankled. "It wasn't until junior high school that it started to settle in on me."

The military seemed a logical option as it followed a kind of family tradition and his personal "romantic dream about being out in the world. All of us, except my youngest brother, were in the military. I took to it immediately when I arrived there. I did three years, eight months, and ten days in all, but it took me a year and a half to get disabused of my romantic notions about it. I got into it and the reality of the military was a turnoff. I learned that the military is the place for people who don't want to think for themselves."

He also learned that soldiers were not immune from racism. One conversation in particular has stuck with him through the years.

"He told me all the things he had heard about, you know, just awful stuff to think about people. And in his last line—and that was, *You're cleaner than I am.* I thought, well, okay. Fine. That's one that sticks with me, that, you know, he's raised up to think that I was some kind of animal."

Morgan had entered the service entertaining visions of being a jet fighter pilot, "making strafing runs over the enemies of my country— with a scarf flung around my neck and a song in my heart. My value system was put in place by the movies," Morgan explains.

I believed what I saw. By sixteen, I was flying my desk up to 18,000 feet . . . while my teacher was drawing on the blackboard. Then I was allowed to get into a jet airplane.

They had the planes lined up on the flight line, and they let us crawl into them. It was a T-33 jet trainer. I sat there looking at all those switches and dials and I got the distinct feeling that I was sitting in the nose of a bomb. I realized my fantasies of flying and fighting were just that—fantasies. They had nothing to do with the reality of killing people. What I wanted was the movie version.

I don't know how long I sat there, but while I was there I had one of those life-changing epiphanies. I realized that I didn't want to do this for a living; I wanted to pretend to do this for a living.

The irony is that even if Freeman still had wanted to be a pilot, his race would have made that difficult. Despite high testing scores, he was summarily assigned to work as a radar mechanic until his discharge in 1959. "I don't know what else it could have been but race," he observed later. "The Air Force was not ready then to encourage a black fighter pilot. But that kind of discouragement is not what stops you from doing it, that's just something to overcome."

Freeman thought the Air Force would be a fair fountainhead of opportunity. Instead it was a reminder that racism was just as much an ingrained institutional problem as it was individual ignorance. With a career in the military thoroughly out of his system,

That was the end of the whole idea of doing anything other than acting for me. I've never had any other vocation.

I've always been a showoff. And that's what acting is, a chance for you to stand up and say, Hey folks, look at me! Look at what I can do!

I'm born to do this, like Picasso was born to paint. Now I'm not comparing myself to Picasso, but, you know, there are some things that just come easy to you. If you're a writer, you're a writer. And if you wait tables or wash cars or fix cars, you go home at night and you write. Whether you do something else is not the point; you write. Painters paint. Actors act.

But Freeman would have to travel many miles and wait many years to fulfill his dream of showcasing that potential on the big screen.

2

WITH HIS MILITARY service a quickly fading blip on his mental horizon, Freeman headed to Hollywood with his few meager belongings and limited cash. "It was just serendipity that I spent almost my whole time after basic training and school in California. I was just right where I needed to be."

He stepped off the bus with unlimited hopes and unrealistic expectations. "I thought I'd just present myself and be hired," he says wryly, recalling the first time he showed up at Paramount Studios wearing his best suit and a brown pork-pie hat. At least, he thought he was at Paramount.

"In February of 1961 I got out there, went to Paramount, told them I was there and what I wanted to do, and they gave me this form to fill out: *How many office machines can you use? How many words can you type a minute?* I was in the wrong place. I thought I was in the studio and I was just in a downtown office."

That was his first clue he might not have been as prepared as he hoped.

I knew what I wanted to do in my teens—that wasn't the question. The question was, how? There's a maze between here and there. It's not a straight line at all. I figured a school situation was the wisest thing. I had no money and no prospects for making any. Then I got a job with the board of education. A few weeks later, I learned that I could go to school at Los Angeles Community College free of charge. They also had a better theater department than the reigning school at the time, the Pasadena Playhouse. I couldn't afford tuition there and didn't have a car, anyway. So I enrolled in acting classes.

LACC is an urban college, situated on Vermont Avenue, a main north-south thoroughfare that is the unofficial eastern edge of Hollywood. Freeman lived in South Central, the Los Angeles counterpart to Chicago's South Side. Located southeast of downtown, South Central was not just a cultural world apart from Hollywood but also geographically isolated. Getting around the city in any timely efficient manner would prove almost as challenging as finding an acting job.

Even though Freeman could catch a bus up Vermont and be dropped off directly across the street from LACC's minicampus, he would then have to take several busses to get to his job at UCLA—traveling through Hollywood, West Hollywood, and Beverly Hills to the sprawling university tucked in the low rolling hills of the Westwood neighborhood of Los Angeles.

"This town almost killed me," he admits. "It's spread all over. The bus system is zoned, and you pay a fare in each zone. From where I was living it was eight zones to school and work. So I did a lot of walking to economize. The police don't like to see pedestrians in certain areas. They watch you very carefully," especially if said pedestrian happens to have dark skin.

It was during this time that Morgan learned to be frugal, "almost to a fault. If I'm making 25 cents, I'm putting away a nickel somewhere."

Despite having been the big fish in his high school's thespian pond, Freeman realized that the movies attracted the best and brightest talent from all over the country. Since he wasn't matinee idol handsome in the vein of Harry Belafonte or Sidney Poitier—the undisputed leading black actors in Hollywood during the 1950s—Morgan knew he needed to distinguish himself through sheer talent. He wasn't trained as an actor. Freeman says he learned to act in large part by watching great actors, such as Jimmy Stewart, when he was growing up, and he knew he needed to better learn his craft.

He had enrolled in LACC's drama program to hone his natural skills but quickly floundered and ended up nearly washing out of the course.

"I didn't think because I was flunking that I couldn't act. I thought that I was flunking because I didn't know what they wanted. Things come naturally to me, though they don't overlay easily. In the acting class community, I found myself doing scene work so far removed from my own life experiences that I was never going to get it. *Othello?* No. Give me something basic."

Even today Freeman says he follows no particular school of acting, preferring natural to any method. "I read Stanislavsky . . . but that business of peeling away layers of skin was too murky and deep for me. I haven't found that I've had to do that in any intellectual sense. What I do, I do intuitively. It just comes easy for me."

His difficulties in the acting classes were balanced by encouragement from other instructors. "I was told that I was good in my dance-movement classes and that I should concentrate on dance because it would enhance my ability to get acting work. But I was twenty-two before I took my first dance class. I had never been athletic, so I was very stiff; I still am. I think what I got mostly from dance was carriage."

The classes also help rid Freeman of his thick southern accent. "We made tapes when we first got there and then again at the end of semester, and we heard the difference in our voices. All during this period, people are telling me how my voice is changing—*your speech is so wonderful . . . it's so mellifluous*—which just increases my desire to speak well and correctly. By the time I got out of there, I was really rounding out the ovals and hitting the final consonants and sounding real good."

But what he got mostly out of Los Angeles that first stay was an understanding that if he was to get any real experience, it probably wasn't going to be in films.

"I got a good running start towards *The Wall*—get down, not going to let anything stop me—but the wall was brick. So when I bounced, I bounced all the way to New York and got onto the stage and stayed there."

His decision that Broadway might be a better bet was made for reasons both personal and professional.

"I moved to New York because I was running away from here, Los Angeles," Freeman laughs. "I met a woman, got in trouble, and I had to get out of here. It was a great theater scene in New York. Ivan Dixon was there, Lou Gossett was there, and of course, Sidney Poitier was the biggest thing going. New York was just more hospitable to black actors then. Hell, it was more hospitable to any kind of actor."

Years later he was ask to list the three smartest things he had done in his life. Freeman announced, "Being born, leaving the Air Force to go to Hollywood, and leaving Hollywood to go to New York."

To support his audition habit, he signed up with a temp agency and got a job first with a talent agent and then as a telegrapher in the telegraph office. "I learned to type in the Air Force, and could type at least sixty-five words a minute. What we did at the telegraph office was called press wireless, sort of a central clearing house for foreign correspondents. Guys from around the world would send us their news stories and we would send them out."

He made enough money to buy a used white Ford convertible. While the car "suddenly made me attractive to women," it did little to jump start Freeman's stage career. Restless, he drove back to the West Coast in 1961 but this time headed to San Francisco where his affinity for dance was again singled out.

"My teacher in stage movement said I really had a feel for dance, and that I should pursue that as a career. So I leaped in, and quickly got in over my head."

So he added tap to his acting classes, determined to somehow create an opportunity. That opportunity came courtesy of the Opera Ring repertory company, which staged musical revivals. Finally, Freeman says, "That's where things started to happen."

Over the next few years he was a background performer in *Can-Can* and Office Krupke in a production of *West Side Story*. His first significant role was in Bertolt Brecht and Kurt Weill's *Threepenny Opera* as the Streetsinger, a recalcitrant town crier who daily announces the unsavory criminal deeds of Soho's notorious "Mack the Knife," which earned Freeman the first positive reviews of his career.

Years later Freeman recalled the challenges of performing in a Brecht play. "Brecht, as you know, is often just a long series of monologues and if it's your monologue, fine, great, go crazy—but if it's not your monologue then you're just standing on stage trying not to upstage but also having nothing to do. So it was during my time doing Brecht that I taught myself how to roll cigarettes. I got myself a bag of tobacco and that's what I did for minutes and minutes on stage was roll my cigarette."

But his tenure at the Opera Ring would come to an abrupt end. The director of *Little Mary Sunshine* was offended when Freeman refused the role of an Indian who waves a flag at the end of the production. "So I was out of a job. It was very depressing."

He snapped out of his funk when one of his dance classmates, who was from Paris, floated the idea of returning to France to establish a chain of dance studios in Europe. Freeman was eagerly in.

"I got my passport, went to work at the post office for six months to earn my fare and was ready to go on to Paris when I reached New York. That was in 1963. I never left."

Swallowing that disappointment, Morgan regrouped. He got his first tantalizing taste of life on a movie set an as extra on Sidney Lumet's *The Pawnbroker*, which was shot on location in Manhattan and Long Island. Starring Rod Steiger, Brock Peters, and Geraldine Fitzgerald and based on the novel by Edward Lewis Wallant, the film is one of the first films to examine the long-term emotional fallout suffered by concentration camp survivors.

The following year Freeman finally got his first professional East

Coast gig as a member of the Cabaret Union. "I remember I went to this audition being run by Michael Kidd, and it was a cattle call. The kind of thing where they go, *okay, I pick you . . . you . . . and you. The rest of you, thank you very much.* And it was for Water World, for the 1964 World's Fair in New York. And it was great. And after that, when the money ran out, and it did pretty quickly, I had to get a job."

Freeman had no false pride when it came to work—he'd do whatever someone would pay him for. More difficult was asking for help when jobs were scarce and money for food even scarcer. He recalls sometimes going for days without eating until he broke down and asked friends for help.

More often than not, though, he was able to find employment—holding down the typical gamut of struggling-actor positions, including manning a take-out counter at Lee's, which Freeman says, "was like working at McDonald's. The worse thing I ever did because . . . it didn't pay at all and they wouldn't let you get tips. I got the job after I had done my first real card-carrying professional job as a dancer, and that show closed and I couldn't get anything else, so I had to wind up going to work at Lee's and I remember one night, one of the dancers that I had worked with, a guy named Bob, who came in and got a hot dog and saw me behind the counter and said what are you doing here?"

Freeman hated it and went back to work as an office temp. "I was very good at them because I was so handy." So much so, there was a point Freeman considered working full time, tempted by the weekly paycheck. "One of my bosses, who really loved me, told me why she couldn't bring me on the regular staff. She said, *"You're gonna go off and audition for parts, and you need that flexibility, and that's fine with me. But if you get a job, you'd be out of here and never look back."*

"I said, 'That's true.' But she also said, 'You're bored to death when there's nothing to do.' And that's because I just can't make work if there's nothing to do. If there's nothing to do, I believe in doing nothing. Now, if there's work to do, I'm on it. I'm all over it, because there is no bad job."

But Freeman also knew that if he was to be a professional actor, he needed to pursue it without a safety net.

I remember making a decision that I was either going to do this or die. It was in 1965. I was maybe twenty-eight. In order to keep living, you have to work at something. Most of us were working in places like restaurants, or we'd drive cabs. I was an office temp. And one day I said, I cannot keep doing this, I cannot.

I was on unemployment at the time. And I told them at the unemployment office, you're ruining my life forcing me to be an office worker when I'm an actor. So they said okay, and stamped my unemployment book. They said okay, you've got six months. Go be an actor. I would have done the office work anyway, but it would have taken me a bit longer. So you seldom get where you are without someone reaching out to give you a hand.

Looking back, Freeman says acting wasn't so much an obsession as it was a necessity. "You do it because that's what you do. That's what defines you. What would you do if you weren't doing what you love, think about that. It's not just what you want to do. It's what you have to do. I rest my case."

He also believes some of his trouble with securing acting jobs came from within, "because you've got to have threads, connecting tissues somewhere, and I didn't have anything to connect me."

His first goal was to concentrate on acting roles rather than dance. He worked as an extra on the largely forgotten film titled *A Man Called Adam*, a Rat Pack–esque vehicle for Sammy Davis Jr. that featured Ossie Davis, Cicely Tyson, and Lola Falana, as well as Peter Lawford, and Frank Sinatra Jr. Freeman must have been in his element on the jazz-flavored set, which boasted appearances by Louis Armstrong and Mel Torme.

In his *New York Times* review, Bosley Crowther applauds the film's diversity—a harbinger of what Freeman's career would one day come to exemplify.

Few film dramas these days bother to explore the world of jazz musicians. . . . Almost as provocative as the theme—a king trumpeter's decline—is the heartening fact that the movie not only stars a Negro artist but also has both Negro and white players in key roles, another rarity. Designed by the star's new movie company . . . this Embassy Pictures presentation rates credit for pluck. Sadly, as a human story it seldom matches the background.

In 1966, Freeman was hired for a "bus and truck tour" of *The Royal Hunt of the Sun*, a dramatic recounting of Pizarro's brutal conquest of the Incas. The Broadway production had the curious casting of David Carradine as Inca king Atahualpa and Christopher Plummer as Pizarro, but the touring company was populated by rank-and-file actors.

Written by Peter Shaffer—who is better known for *Equus* and *Amadeus*—the play is epic in scope and staging. Freeman did double duty as a member of the Inca chorus and as an understudy for one of the speaking roles.

"One night we were in Des Moines, and I got to go on," he recalls. "It was so easy. The feeling of rightness and power that washed over me on the stage that night came as a revelation to me. I said to myself, 'This is what you do; *this* is where you really shine.'"

Freeman says that through his life, beginning with his birth, years ending in seven have tended to be significant. The year 1967 followed that pattern. "It was a banner year for me. It was when I first learned to sail, got on my first eighteen-foot boat. It was also the year when I had the thunderbolt of realization: I'm not a dancer. I'm not an office worker. I'm an actor."

He made his off-Broadway debut at the Orpheum Theater in 2 one-acts by George Tabori—*The Demonstration* and *Man and Dog*—controversially titled *The Niggerlovers*. The plays were inspired by the 1961 effort of "freedom riders" to force an end to segregation on southern buses and trains after the Supreme Court had deemed such practices unconstitutional. His costars included Stacey Keach and Viveca Lindfors. The show only ran for twenty-five performances but put some much needed cash in Freeman's pocket.

Despite the close-to-home subject matter of the plays, Morgan wasn't at all making a political statement—it was about the work and the $72 a week paycheck. "I was just trying to stay alive in New York. It was wonderful. I wasn't hungry anymore, and neither was my dog. And I walked out of that into *Hello Dolly!*"

Hello Dolly! starring Carol Channing as matchmaker Dolly Levi, originally opened at the St. James Theater in January 1964 and won a bushel basket of Tony Awards, including best musical, best score, and a best lead actress in a musical award for Channing.

In late 1967, an all-black production was mounted as a vehicle for Pearl Bailey; Freeman was cast as the head waiter—putting to good use all his dance training. He would be with the show for almost a year which give Freeman a steady income from acting for the first time as well as priceless experience. "It was . . . a training ground like no other. I worked on that show for eleven months with Pearl, and in that eleven months, what I watched every show was a total professional, hundred and ten percent every time out."

From Pearl Bailey he "learned how to be a professional, how to do things with grace and respect for everyone onstage and backstage."

For the rest of the decade Freeman found steady theater work between workshop productions, regional theater, and off-Broadway. He also became involved with the New York Shakespeare Festival. Years later, the festival's producer, Joseph Papp, remembered the six-foot two-inch Freeman made quite an impression back in the day. "He had very good speech, bore himself with a certain grace and looked like a king."

Not every stage experience was one for the ages, however. Freeman says the worst role he ever performed was in a play on Broadway he chooses not to name. "It was a three character play—would-be comedy—and I think the funniest thing about it was at one night the lead actor just completely forgot every line. It was one of those situations where you can't help. You can't throw him a line, you can't suggest a way for him to get out of it, you can't do anything—it's his problem."

But even the bad experiences only served to make him better. He wasn't famous but Freeman was a working actor, and to him that meant a certain measure of success. "I was doing fine. I always figure a good living for an actor is not having to wait tables," which is why, "every job was a big step."

Freeman felt secure enough to get married in 1967 to Jeanette Bradshaw, whom he had met when they worked in the same travel agency. He adopted Jeanette's daughter, Deena, from a previous relationship, and together they had Morgana, who was born in 1971.

Despite all the theater work, Freeman's ultimate goal remained movies, and he finally cracked the door with a role in the children's film *Who Says I Can't Ride a Rainbow?* a feel-good docudrama about neighborhood efforts to save a Greenwich Village petting zoo from developers who want to use the property for a housing complex and the local kids' plan to save a pony named Rainbow from ending up dog food. Freeman played a character named Afro.

While not exactly the film debut he might have wished for, it was still valuable experience, even if it didn't make him a lot of money. For someone so passionate to act in movies, the early 1970s must have been like dying of thirst in the middle of an ocean. Starting with *Watermelon Man* in 1970 and followed by box office hits *Shaft* and *Superfly,* "blaxploitaton" films became Hollywood's newest genre, targeted specifically at the black urban audience. Not only were the casts largely black but also the soundtracks incorporated black artists such as Isaac Hayes and Curtis Mayfield.

These movies shamelessly presented exaggerated stereotypes of both races, which brought ire and indignation from sober-minded civil rights organizations and the embrace of black audiences starved to see any incarnation of themselves on film. But for those on the front lines of the civil rights struggle, the films irresponsibly propagated negative images of blacks. The nations' most powerful black organizations, including the Urban League, the National Association for the Advancement of Colored People, and the Southern Christian Leadership Conference, formed the Coalition against Blaxploitation which effectively snuffed out the genre by the decade's end.

In 1990, Lena Horne wrote an essay in *Ebony* expressing her disappointment in both Hollywood's stereotyping—and ultimate dismissal—of black talent.

"If the most important thing to happen for Blacks in this century was the Civil Rights Movement, the film industry's dismal follow-up to it was simply to show a whole new range of Black stereotypes: the pimp, hustler, addict, rogue cop, hooker," she observed.

Thus during the seventies we had a decade of so-called "blaxploitation" films. Many fine actors and actresses were employed in these films, which finally created jobs for Black directors and technicians. Several of these pictures were top-grossing hits, but few had any lasting value, and much of what they portrayed saddled us for a time with negative images we are still trying to undo. However, White Hollywood, which had produced most of the blaxploitation pictures, and reaped the profits from them, adapted the winning formula of the Black action picture to create a whole new cycle of White action pictures, which is still running today. In the process, the Black films were phased out and once again, Black performers found less and less work.

But in 1970, all Freeman saw was other black actors flooding the West Coast, and he wanted to join them. "All the New York actors were going to Hollywood, starring in it, making $40,000. I said to my agent whose name was Jeff Hunter, picked me up from the first stage play I did in New York. I said, 'Everybody's going out there and they're working. I'm sitting here languishing. I should go—don't you think I should go out to Hollywood?'"

But Jeff Hunter urged restraint. "His advice to me was, 'I don't think so. When they want you, they'll send for you.' It worked—though they didn't want me for a long time. "

So Freeman heeded the advice and instead took a job in television on a PBS children's show. Produced by the Children's Television Workshop, the program was created for kids who had outgrown CTW's preschool phenomenon, *Sesame Street*. *The Electric Company's* mandate was to improve math and reading skills for the primary school set, through sketch comedy and then state-of-the-art computer graphics.

Freeman was cast as the ultra hip Easy Reader, an obvious—and intentional—play on *Easy Rider*. "But he was a junkie for reading," explains Paul Dooley, the show's head writer. Dooley, a comic actor who would go on to become a familiar face to both television and film audiences, said, "We did things for the adults that kids might not get, but it didn't cost us anything. *The Electric Company* had a hip-ness about it. We were told never to look or sound anything like *Sesame Street*. We did-n't want some six-year-old kid to say, *'I'm not going to watch that, that's just like Sesame Street! That's for little kids!'*"

In addition to Easy Reader, Freeman played other characters including radio DJ Mel Mounds, The Cop, a Mad Scientist, and Count Dracula. With regular guests including Rita Moreno, Bill Cosby, and Bugs Bunny voice-over artist Mel Blanc, the show was an immediate hit.

Freeman says his now-signature voice evolved over the years, in part thanks to the series. Earlier in his career he says, "Like many people, I spoke at a higher register than my voice actually is. Now, that's okay for women because it sounds feminine but I had to learn to bring it down. I spoke much faster. I really got control over it doing all of those voice-overs I had to do on *Electric Company*. It's why I've always said there are no bad jobs."

A long-running television series is the ultimate security for a journeyman actor. While it can be powerfully seductive, it can also be emotionally and professionally constricting. Freeman still yearned to break into movies with challenging dramatic roles, but he had to balance that passion with the realities of needing to support his family. Film roles were nonexistent, and there wasn't enough theater work, either, to justify quitting, so instead he stayed and wallowed.

"I could hardly stand to get up in the morning and go to work. That was part of the whole success syndrome and part of the whole frustration of being trapped by greed and insecurity—the actor's constant bane. *Ah*, you tell yourself, *this is absolutely the last year I'm going to do this.*"

He might have been miserable but he never let it seep into his performance. Luis Avalos, who played Igor opposite Freeman's Mad Scientist, has nothing but glowing memories of working together. "He's a wonderful singer, great dancer, and terrific actor. Even doing skits, one can tell the weight of an actor."

But with the stress and fatigue of churning out a weekly show and the concern he was whoring his potential, Freeman felt as if he were treading water in purgatory and began drowning in his unhappiness. "I'm not an alcoholic or anything but . . . I started going around the bend."

By the mid-1970s, Freeman's drinking got out of control. "You start off going to lunch and having a martini, and then you have two martinis because you can do it, and then you go home and have two or three scotches because you can do it. But next thing I knew I was going through two or three quarts of whiskey a week, which may not be a lot to people who really drink, but it was too much for me. I remember waking up once in my doorway, where I had fallen down. And I lay there thinking, *You're lying face down, drunk, and this will never do.*"

In 1998, Freeman was quoted in the London *Mirror* by reporter Thomas Quinn saying, "My marriage was breaking up and I hated my job—I was in a TV show too long and wanted out. I wanted to do something different and I'm pretty determined when I have to be. But what I really needed was something that could break that mould of drinking and drinking. So I quit alcohol, went cold turkey—and started to smoke marijuana."

Freeman added, "Do you remember Woodstock? The air was heavy with ganja but there wasn't one fight. It is not a drug that's conducive to aggression; it's a great chill-out. Of course, you can misuse it. If you don't have a sense of moderation, then you are going to pay for it."

Also helping Freeman regain his balance was a different kind of flying. "I'd bought a boat in 1967 and I give it all the credit for giving me back control of my life. I'd always wanted to fly, and not until I saw the wings of sailboats did I understand the flying I could do."

By the time *The Electric Company* went off the air in October 1977, they had shot 780 episodes. Coming into people's home every weekday morning—*Easy Reader, that's my name; Reading, writing, that's my game*—for nearly six years made Freeman a familiar face to kids and their parents everywhere . . . and for decades afterward.

"One of my nightmares is that I'm this old, old, old guy and somebody about fifty years old comes up to me and says, *Easy Reader, right?* It's like being known as Captain Kangaroo." Particularly irksome for Freeman is "when I meet people who are parents now who talk about how they grew up with me."

Morgan's annoyance is probably more indicative of his emotional state at the time than lack of appreciation. "I've seen reruns of it once or twice. It's exactly like time travel. It's thirty years old now. It was a very creative show, but man, it was a long gig. I was fried. And I hated myself for not having the courage to just walk away. But then it ended, and I had to find something else to do—lucky for me."

What he found was *The Mighty Gents*, a grim look at the members of a black Newark high school street gang fifteen years later, now grown men with no hope for ever changing their lot in life. Freeman played an old, disillusioned wino named Zeke, on whom the group takes out their frustrations.

The play, originally called *The Last Street Play*, was initially presented off-Broadway at the Manhattan Theater Club. But rave reviews convinced James Lipton—writer, director, novelist, and now host of *Inside the Actor's Studio*—to find backers to move the drama to Broadway.

During its five-week pre-Broadway run in Washington, D.C., *Washington Post* reviewer Richard Coe noted, "Author Richard Wesley perceives, within a Newark, N.J., black ghetto, some of the timeless form and formality of Greek tragedy. To the Greeks, life boiled down to what the Fates demanded. Wesley is less passive. He sees, in values and misplaced values, how man's choices can be an active force."

But when the play opened on April 16, 1978, at the Ambassador Theater, New York critics were less kind. Freeman believes Broadway was the wrong place for something strong. "It should've stayed where it was, instead of moving to a big house, where it closed in a little more than a week. Broadway wouldn't support heavy work like that, even back in those days."

Part of the disappointment was his affection for the character. "Zeke is one of those guys who is still holding on. His fingernails are broken, down to the quick. But he still has a grip. You look at those people where I live who would go on the nickel and deteriorate, and Zeke has this hand that shakes and goes crazy, and he would check into a complete stupor. But then in the morning, with all of New City stepping over him to get to work, what does he think about? *Hey, you got a dime?* It was great to play that. It was great to think that. It was great to go there."

Even though the play closed after only nine performances, it brought Freeman front and center, earning him a Tony nomination and the Drama Desk Award as Outstanding Featured Actor in a play. In addition, Actors' Equity named the forty-year-old actor Best Male Newcomer of the season.

Freeman took the accolades very much to heart. "I thought I was ready and here it came. But the play closed in a week and it sort of faded away."

Even so, "the noise was all around me, and I really got into the lifestyle. I was living over my head, using up my credit cards, and, man, I got in debt fast."

The recognition that seemed to portend bigger and better roles was in fact the start of a demoralizing two-year film lull. But one of the early highlights of Freeman's career occurred that year when Freeman got the opportunity to work with Jose Ferrer, who Morgan had admired since seeing him play Cyrano De Bergerac.

I got a call, September of 1978 . . .
Morgan?
Yeah?
It's Jose Ferrer.
And I said, "*Who?*"—but I knew it was him, man, nobody had a voice like his voice. He wanted me to do a two-act play with him and when he asked I said, kinda falsetto, *Yeah.*

I mean this is my hero and he's calling me to work with him and here I am, living in New Jersey. I drove right to New York and we did this play. But you know, in the second week of rehearsal he pulled me aside, set me down and said, "*You've got to get over this worship,*" 'cause we couldn't do that play with me making all these worshipful eyes at him all the time. But you know, he was . . . he could act, man. It was a pinch-me moment. I couldn't believe— still can't believe—that it happened.

Even if Hollywood wasn't calling, his theater work continued to gain notice and recognition. He appeared in a thirteen-performance Public Theater production of Shakespeare's *Coriolanus* in 1979 and won an OBIE in 1980 for his turn in *Mother Courage* and *Coriolanus*. (The OBIEs are presented by *The Village Voice* and were established in 1956 to acknowledge and support off-Broadway theater.)

But the meager salaries of theater in general, and off-Broadway in particular, didn't stretch very far. Soon, Freeman was again an out-of-work actor with few prospects.

His long-troubled marriage finally buckled under the strain and ended in divorce. Frustrated and emotionally eroded from the endless struggle to get ahead, Freeman considered finding full-time employment somewhere. But he would be saved from such spiritual suicide by the unlikely pairing of Robert Redford and a pimp named Fast Black.

3

FREEMAN'S FIRST IMPORTANT film role came courtesy of Robert Redford in the prison drama *Brubaker*. Besides the normal built-in prerelease buzz Redford brought to the project, there was added media interest because the movie was based on the real life exploits of Warden Tom Murton.

In February 1967, Murton was appointed superintendent of the Arkansas Prison System, a state with a long history of penal corruption. The practice of convict leasing had started before the Civil War and its original intent was economic. Leasing out groups of inmates to the private sector—whether it be local farms and plantation or businesses— was done as a cost saving measure to the state. In exchange, the prisoners were to be treated humanely and given adequate food and shelter. But the many contractors regularly beat and starved the inmates. Wardens and officials were paid to look the other way—an action resulting in numerous scandals.

The practice was finally outlawed after Governor George W. Donaghey who pardoned 360 prisoners at the end of his term. The state prison population was slashed by a third, leaving barely enough inmates to work the state's own correctional farms. The Arkansas General Assembly followed suit and two months later, in February 1913, formally outlawed convict leasing.

However, other corruptions replaced the leasings and Murton was appointed warden with a mandate to clean up the notorious prison farms that were suspected of meting out punishment unconstitutionally cruel and unusual.

Murton soon locked horns with the very governor who appointed him after claiming three human skeletons found at Cummins were of inmates who had been tortured and beaten to death by prison officials and buried to cover up the crime. Although Murton was fired by Governor Winthrop Rockefeller in March 1968, a subsequent investigation corroborated Murton's claims. The most shocking was the revelation that "a prison hospital served as torture chamber and a doctor as chief tormentor."

According to Murton's book, *Accomplices to the Crime*, prisoners had needles driven under their fingernails, were strapped to an operating table, and had wires attached to their genitals. Then someone would generate electricity by using a hand crank telephone, which became known as the Tucker Telephone, to generate over 100 volts.

In 1970, District Court Judge J. Smith Henley declared the Arkansas prison system unconstitutional and ordered the State Corrections Board to revamp it. The Eighth Circuit Court of Appeals also ordered the abolishment of corporal punishment.

Tom Murton went on to be a tenured professor of criminology at the University of Minnesota and served as an expert consultant on *Brubaker*.

The film takes a few dramatic liberties, such as Redford going undercover as an inmate to witness the horrific conditions and brutality at the prison farms—all of which is graphically depicted. After he reveals his true identity, he sets about trying to install reforms and finds himself butting heads with both state and local officials and townspeople who have benefited from the illegal convict leasing and corruption at the prison farm.

Freeman plays an inmate named Walter. When asked what special preparation he did for the role, the answer was brief—none. "Acting the part of someone who's incarcerated doesn't require any specific knowledge of incarceration because men don't change. Once you're in that situation, you just toe whatever line you have to toe."

In what would become a recurring theme in his career, Freeman rose above the somewhat clichéd script to give the film bite and humanity. *New Yorker's* Pauline Kael, arguably one of the nation's most influential movie critics, singled out his performance, noting, "As a death-row prisoner who broke out of his hole and started to strangle another convict, he gave [*Brubaker*] a sudden charge that the moviemakers didn't seem to know what to do with." She would go on to say that once Freeman's character leaves, the film never recovers.

And yet, important roles that would move him up the Hollywood ladder failed to follow, although he continued to get film work. He played a police detective in the modestly successful mystery thriller *Eyewitness* which starred Sigourney Weaver and William Hurt. He played Malcolm X in the low budget drama *Death of a Prophet*. Despite the breathless marketing blurb, "This incredible film follows the events in the final twenty four hours of the life of controversial religious and political leader Malcolm X. Fanatics tried to firebomb his home. They tried to murder him white he slept. Why was he so hated? Where were the police on the day of his assassination? How did his killers manage to escape?" the film was thoughtful and sober—perhaps too much so—and quickly disappeared from theaters.

Once again in dire need of money, Freeman agreed to join a daytime soap. *Another World* was one of the doyennes of daytime serials and the first to adopt the hour format. Debuting in 1964, the sudser followed the scandals, schemes, and seductions of the residents of Bay City, Illinois.

For one year and seven months, Freeman played architect Roy Bingham—after convincing the producers it was a better character name than the originally planned "George Washington Jones." For a man who once said there was no such thing as a bad job, his soap stint wasn't particularly fruitful, either—except to reaffirm that daytime wasn't his job of choice.

"You learn it's not what you want to do, that's what you learn. It was satisfying in that when I got the job I had no job and I needed one in sort of a desperate way. I don't want to push it down too low, but for me it was not satisfying work. What was satisfying to me was the paycheck."

Theater continued to feed his creative soul. He was cast as the lead in the off-Broadway musical *The Gospel at Colonus*, at the Guthrie Theater which was adapted from Sophocles' *Oedipus at Colonus* and earned his second OBIE in 1984.

He stayed with the soap for two patience-straining years until he was written out after Bingham got married and never returned from his honeymoon. The plot line was rather ironic as Freeman would himself once again be a newlywed. On June 16, 1984, he married costume designer Myrna Colley-Lee. They originally met during an off-Broadway play in 1976 when Freeman was on the skids from drinking and his relationship with Jeanette Bradshaw unraveling. Myrna admits it wasn't exactly love at first sight. "He was very aloof, alone. It turned out he was separating from his wife, so he was very melancholy." She also notes that a factor in him going cold-turkey from drinking was that it hit a little too close to home. "Thinking about his father made him stop."

By the time they wed, Freeman was already the father of four children, three of them adults, but Myrna longed to raise a child of her own. "I was hysterical to have a baby," she admits, acknowledging Morgan "didn't want another." Then Colley-Lee says fate intervened. "His daughter Deena was having a hard time, so I asked for E'Dena [her daughter] to live with us. Morgan functions more like a grandfather, but he's happy I got this chance at parenting."

Freeman was also happy to get back on the movie saddle. Paul Newman hired Freeman for his first role in three years when he cast him in *Harry & Son*.

The review by the *Boston Globe's* Jay Carr sums up the general reaction to the film.

Harry and Son wants to be a love story between father and son, but doesn't know how to build to its frequent Big Moments. It just lurches from one to the next until the film, which initially promised an interesting blue-collar texture, finally seems to vaporize and reconstitute itself as a series of TV sitcom chunks. Harry plays a joke on his greedy daughter. Howard deliberately loses a string of pedestrian jobs so he can keep writing. Harry is conveniently introduced by Howard to a sexually (and instantly) voracious secretary, an ungrateful role assigned to Judith Ivey. It's the kind of movie in which nobody does anything much about Harry's obvious cardiac symptoms, more, it seems, out of a reluctance to give up that big scene than out of any macho imperative.

Rita Kempley of *The Washington Post* is more succinct. "Paul Newman and Robby Benson come down with Terminal Endearment in *Harry & Son*, a love story for guys with quiche on their breath.

"No trees were killed to make this movie. It's composed entirely of recycled platitudes. And the point, other than that tomorrow is the first day of the rest of your life, is to Put on a Happy Face. It was shot in Florida, but it's pure California. Mellow between the ears."

Perhaps the best things that can be said is that nobody seemed to even notice Freeman was in the film, which would rank as little more than a much-needed payday and a chance to work with Newman in the grander scheme of Morgan's life. Over the next several years, Freeman worked his way through several more forgettable feature and TV films—*Teachers, Marie, Execution of Raymond Graham, That Was Then . . . This Is Now, Resting Place, Fight for Life,* and Showtime's *Clinton and Nadine.*

The most notable project was the controversial CBS miniseries, *The Atlanta Child Murders.* In the summer of 1979, youngsters in Atlanta began disappearing at at terrifying clip. It began with the disappearance of two boys. In the early hours of July 21, fourteen-year-old Edward Hope Smith left a skating rink after a date with his girlfriend and headed for home on foot. He never made it. A few days larer, his friend Alfred Evans, also fourteen, left home to go see a movie. He was never seen again.

On July 28, in a secluded wooded area in southwestern Atlanta, the bodies of both boys were found. Hope had been killed with a .22 caliber, and the medical examiner suspected the other boy had been strangled. Edward's socks and shirt were missing, and Alfred was wearing a belt that didn't belong to him.

Two more boys disappeared in November, first fourteen-year-old Milton Harvey, then Yusef Bell who a witness reported seeing getting into a blue car—a clue police initially dismissed. Jeffery Mathis, ten, was last seen by a friend getting into a blue car. After that, as the bodies piled up, police began to suspect many of the deaths were related.

In all, over an approximate two-year period twenty-nine children would be murdered, and the man believed responsible, Wayne Williams, had been convicted based solely on circumstantial and forensic evidence. He is serving life imprisonment.

Many in the black community believed Williams had been a scapegoat for a beleaguered police force under extreme pressure to stop a perceived serial killer. Others argued that it was doubtful any single killer was responsible for all the deaths.

It was clear from Abby Mann's script that he fell on the side of those who questioned Williams's guilt. Freeman and James Earl Jones play two police detectives—Lieutenant Ben Shelter and Major Jake Walker—who carry the action in the first half of the mini, which focuses on the investigation. The second half is the trial.

Both Freeman's and Jones's characters are fictitious composites, but many of the real investigators involved in the murders took exception to the "facts" depicted in the docudrama, especially in the courtroom sequence. While Mann claimed the testimony was taken directly from transcripts, it was selective testimony.

Although suspected of more murders, Williams was tried for the deaths of Nathaniel Cater and Jimmy Ray Payne. *Boston Globe* reporter Joanne Ball outlined the fact versus fiction aspect of the miniseries.

"The prosecution spent days building a case to connect fibers from

Williams' house and car to the two and ten other victims. The film reduced that evidence to one witness who is belittled by defense attorney Alvin Binder (Jason Robards). . . .

"Binder asked prosecution witness Georgia forensic expert Larry Peterson if he had visited the homes of the two victims in analyzing the fibers. When Peterson said he had not, Binder pointed to that as a failing in the prosecution's case. But, according to Joseph J. Drolet, a main prosecutor in the Williams case who was not portrayed in the film . . . the primary expert was Harold Deadman of the FBI who did go to the victims' homes," although that testimony was not included. Another fact deleted from the miniseries was the failure to mention "police found bloodstains in Williams' car that matched two of the victims."

At one point, Lt. Shelter voices doubt about Williams's guilt—a view shared by Freeman.

"They were looking but all they had was the fibers. They couldn't come up with anything but the fibers and this young man."

The fibers were the crux of the prosecution's case because they have a unique weave, were found on two bodies, and matched the carpeting in Williams's home.

"I believe it was a situation where one person was not responsible for all of the killings," Freeman said at the time. "The first two or three, maybe, but not all of them. The show would suggest that Williams was an incredibly smart person to get away with so many killings. He was smart, but not that smart."

Freeman also comments, "After Williams was jailed, the killings continued, but they were not linked to the series of killings."

In between projects, Freeman would frequently head to East Chester Bay in the Bronx where his thirty-foot sloop was docked to indulge his passion for sailing. "When you live in the world of make-believe, you need something real. I go sailing, I'm in the real world."

It says something about how our priorities change as we grow older when Freeman admits, "I used to feel best when I was acting. Now I feel best when I'm sailing. It's a feeling of freedom. Sailing, you spread your own wings."

But growing older doesn't necessarily mean growing tamer. "I like to live on the edge. When I sail, I don't wear a harness or a life preserver. I'd rather drown than be eaten alive."

But soon Freeman would have considerably less time to spend sailing because his career was about to take a dramatic turn on the merits of a most unlikely film, *Street Smart*, and a most unlikely character, Fast Black. At first glance, playing a pimp wouldn't seem to be a natural role for Freeman, who had always been careful not to play stereotypes—one of his reasons for avoiding the blaxploitation era. But he saw this particular character as a chance to break the mold.

"I had no intention of wearing crushed-velvet jump suits, big hats or high-heeled pumps," Freeman says. "The thing with this character was that he wasn't a caricature. I always wanted to play a pimp because I see him differently—a guy who has some power with his life. What a lot of actors resent are these jive characters like the ones on *Baretta* and *Starsky and Hutch*. I wouldn't do that, but I wouldn't pass up this well-written a role."

The film was written by David Freeman, a former journalist and sometime playwright, who became famous for making up his *New Yorker* stories long before Jason Blair left the *New York Times* in disgrace. His most famous "dramatic re-creation" was titled "The Lifestyle of a Pimp." Interestingly, when his fabricating was discovered it barely caused a blip on the national consciousness. Instead, the writer left New York for California, where he landed a high-paying job as a script "rewriter."

Eventually, David wrote a script based on his experiences at the *New Yorker*. In *Street Smart*, Christopher Reeves plays Jonathan Fisher, a Harvard-educated writer who tries to give his career a much-needed boost by pitching a story to his editor about a day in the life of a pimp. The editor loves it. What Fisher failed to mention is that he doesn't know any pimps so he fabricates the story, which garners him a lot of attention and makes him the journalist of the hour.

Unfortunately, the police believe Fisher's source is a pimp they suspect of murder so the journalist is ordered to turn over his notes. If Fisher admits he made the story up, his career is as good as over. If he keeps up the pretense, he may end up in jail. Unfortunately for him, the pimp in question, Fast Black, also believes the magazine article was about him and starts to shadow Fisher, who in turn is attracted to one of Fast Black's girls, played by Kathy Baker.

The film was shepherded to the screen by Reeves, who had been sent the script in 1981 when it was called *Streets of New York*. Several years later he picked it back up, contacted the screenwriter to discuss some revisions and soon the project was green lit.

"I'm frequently offered a lot of money to kill people on screen—to pump up in a gym and blow people away, and I eagerly look for scripts that offer me an alternative," Reeves said shortly after the film's release. "I really had been longing to do either a romantic comedy or something about a guy who wears blue jeans and sneakers."

What made Freeman's role so memorable wasn't as much what he did but what he didn't do, a characterization he based on a real-life observation. "A block away from where I used to live on New York's West Side, there were always these street girls outside, no matter what time of year. Every now and then a pimp would come along, and you'd see him chastise the girls. I saw one guy drag a girl in a hammerlock, just drag her down the street punching her face. He was real quiet about it, too. He wasn't yelling at her at all. Just talking—as he punched her in the face. That's the way you've got to play that character. That's how I put him together."

Freeman says he remembers talking to a pimp he met in Chicago. "He was a procurer, a very seductive man. I remember asking him,

"What do you do?"

"I provide things."

"What?"

"What do you want?"

Freeman continues, "I had no question in my mind that whatever I wanted, he'd get it. All I had to have was the price."

Street Smart was both extremely gratifying and unexpectedly humbling for Freeman, because it was the first time he had the chance to see himself at length on the big screen.

"I grew up on the stage. The big difference is that on the stage I see me through you; I see me through the audience. You are my reflection of my work and I always walk away from the theater expanded. I'm fantastic; I'm really good. Then you do a film. And now you see yourself and you're not so good. I thought I looked better than that, now you all become liars; I cannot trust you, because I know. The big fear is that one day, you're going to know. It's humbling to watch yourself, to see yourself up there."

Although the film came and went within a week or two, Freeman's performance lingered. *Washington Post* reviewer Hal Hinson wrote, "The film's director, Jerry Schatzberg, takes his naive, Harvard-educated hero, who sees himself as privileged, exempt from any real danger—a kind of American princeling—and rubs his nose in the black man's edgy world. As Fast Black, Morgan Freeman is danger incarnate, an unsheathed blade. His performance here is a great one—he seems silky, but there's broken glass underneath. If the rest of the movie had been up to his level it would have been too intense to sit through."

Another *Post* writer, Richard Harrington, added, "The most convincing acting comes from Freeman as the vicious pimp Fast Black. The . . . veteran actor gives his character an indelibly ugly and disturbing edge, making quite real the mix of paternalism and sudden sadism that pimps use to keep their victims on a short leash."

New Yorker movie critic doyenne Pauline Kael, who had also singled Freeman out for *Brubaker*, began her review with the now infamous question. "Is Morgan Freeman America's greatest actor? . . . He turns a haphazardly written Times Square pimp into something so revealing that it's a classic performance." She goes on to describe Fast Black as possessing "a scary, sordid magnetism. He's seductive—he has a veneer of affability—but he's all contradictions; you never know where you are with him except right this minute, and the minute can be cut short."

Costar Christopher Reeves was equally impressed with how deeply Freeman immersed himself, telling an anecdote about a scene that called for Fast Black to hold a broken bottle to Fisher's neck. "On one take, he drew blood. He kept acting, didn't stop, because he's too good for that. But afterwards it took me a half hour to calm him down. He kept saying, "*Oh my God, I cut you*," and apologizing, and I had to laugh. All this sensitivity from a crazed street pimp!"

When asked about his technique and what it is that makes his characters come to such life, Freeman says it's all about the ears.

"I read somewhere, and I think it might have been the book *An Actor Prepares*, that one of the keys to acting is reacting, and in order to react, you have to listen. The big danger in acting is to wait for your line. That's what I never do. I always listen, no matter how many times we do it."

He also credits his costars. "It seems to me that I never grow unless I'm actually working with other actors who have shed whatever shell it is that keeps them insulated from each other."

But while Freeman can explain the craft of acting, explaining the art of it isn't so easy. "It's kind of hard to explain, because I don't do anything. The characters leap off the page; they just come up off the page. If you can see them, there's nothing to playing them. If you can read the script and you see the inside of a character, you know what is motivating the character. After that, all you need is the costumes."

Wardrobe aside, Freeman claims Fast Black is one of his best performances, "Because when I look at it, I see a side of my character that isn't out there—it's not walking out in the open, but it's very definite. I had a great time."

As far as Kael's oft-quoted question, Freeman opts for good-humored modesty. "It's always great when someone sings your praises, but there's a danger zone in believing your own press. I was thrilled when Pauline Kael wrote that. But then, what happens when someone turns around and writes, *This motherfucker ain't shit!* That has happened."

Reviews in general, he says, don't "change anything. It only changes something if I start believing my press. You can't be the greatest anything in acting, because you're too dependent on other people." That said, "it was an excellent thing to read. I think it would have been headier had I been thirty years old. I was fifty and I had been doing this for a while. But you have to really back away from stuff like that, because acting is ensemble. The better I am, the more I have to thank whomever my partners are. It's not a one-man show."

It's somewhat ironic that in later years Freeman would find producers increasingly resistant to cast him as a villain, which is perhaps why Fast Black remains one of his favorite performances. "Bad guys are complex. They can be good, charming, mercurial. They can be hidden, they can be psychotic, they can be schizophrenic. Bad guys have so many reasons and stuff to be bad. The bad psyche is a more interesting study. Why does this guy do this? Where does the anger come from? Is it anger? Or is it just the yin and yang?"

Freeman's *Street Smart* costar, Christopher Reeves died in October 2004, nine years after a horse riding accident left him paralyzed from the neck down. Looking back, Freeman sounds melancholy when talking about Reeves's legacy.

Chris' life was governed by circumstances that spiraled away from him, I think. He was a very passionate actor—he loved a lot of things, he loved the stage, he had a lot of aspirations to film a lot of different things. But then *Superman* came and something happened to him that happens to a lot of actors. He was so wholly swallowed [by] the Superman myth or the myth of Superman that by the time he did *Superman II*, he had completely internalized that image and character. And eventually, I think he realized the lie of that persona, so that when *Superman III* came around as it inevitably must, he did it under some duress.

He had started to desire the old things again—that old passion started to stir him again and he wanted more and more to go against the popular grain or rather, the cast that his popularity had put him in. So he started to desire, more and more, weaker roles— I should say more human parts. So he doesn't want to make [*Superman IV*] at all. He ultimately couldn't resist, the money was stupid, but he held them up so that he could do *Street Smart*. The whole idea of *Street Smart* was one of flawed people.

Freeman says the *Superman* production company was not thrilled with Reeves's character in *Street Smart*.

> They worried about how the public would react to him being human, but that was the point. I met him where he was trying really hard to be human again. He was going back to Williamstown, doing little plays, amateur theater, reintroducing himself to the reasons that he got into acting. He was a different person when I met him than he was I bet even just a few months before.
>
> The accident—and remember he was a pilot, he was a sailor, he lived his life fully—but the accident, he didn't have greatness until that accident. The idea that even this could be overcome: so many people in that situation began to think that if he could overcome, than I could overcome. His activism, his work championing stem-cell research—the way that he became a real citizen of his world and the way that he allowed his life to be opened to the public so that they could see him at his weakest. . . . The accident was a horrible thing—but that horrible thing made Chris, at the end of his life, Superman. It's a happy irony if there is such a thing. I'm proud to have known him.

Unlike the other false starts his career had experienced, the one after *Street Smart* stuck. Freeman would go on to be honored with best supporting actor awards from New York Film Critics, the National Society of Film Critics, the Los Angeles Film Critics, and the Independent Film Project's Spirit Award.

Morgan Freeman had officially arrived—at fifty years old.

> I was known in New York; I was a big name here on the stage but nobody in Hollywood knew me, and that's what Fast Black did. All of a sudden, it was *Who is this guy?*
>
> Making it later in life means you develop a philosophy to explain to yourself why it took so long, and what good was it that it took so long. It took so long because that's the way your karma

works, that's the way it's fated to be. And I think the reason for that is that my guardian angel was hard at work. If you start making large sums of money and you're in your thirties and you're like me, it ain't necessarily a good thing. The indulgence thing can really get out of hand—quick.

Not only was Freeman getting his moment but also were a handful of other black actors and filmmakers such as Denzel Washington, Whoopie Goldberg, and Spike Lee—a happenstance Freeman does not view as coincidental.

I think there was a change of consciousness in the country as a whole around that period, for any number of reasons. It goes back, I think, to the aftermath of the Vietnam War and the advent of the Carter era, which had a softening effect on the country. By 1984, when Jesse Jackson made a credible run for the presidency, the black-exploitation period in the movies had come and gone, and then there was a resurgence of different kinds of stories involving black people. At the same time, the actors' unions were making a push toward open casting. It all reached its zenith with the success of *The Cosby Show.* So a wave began to happen, and we were all lifted with that wave.

Of course, it helped that Freeman was as natural on celluloid as in real life. "I was comfortable in front of a camera from Day One," he says. "I felt more comfortable, in fact, than I had on the stage—and I had never felt uncomfortable on the stage. This is my calling. I was born to do it."

And suddenly he'd be doing a whole lot of it.

4

A<small>T THE SAME</small> time Freeman was busy on the interview circuit promoting *Street Smart*, he was in rehearsal for a new off-Broadway play that he had aggressively pursued. Written by Atlanta-born Alfred Uhry, the play spanned twenty-five years of the relationship between a liberal elderly southern Jewish woman and her black chauffeur, Hoke. It was called *Driving Miss Daisy* and opened April 15, 1987, at Playwrights Horizons. By the summer it had reopened on Broadway at the John Houseman Theater on 42nd Street due to audience demand.

It was Uhry's first play and, like Freeman, he had struggled through an up-and-down career, mostly writing lyrics and librettos for obscure, now-forgotten musicals. His one bright spot before *Daisy* was a 1976 Tony nomination for his work on *The Robber Bridegroom*. For inspiration, he dug deep into his past. Part autobiographical, part memory play, Daisy Werthan was a composite of Uhry's mother, sisters, and grandmother—the latter having had a black chauffeur.

"From what I had seen of Dana's work, I knew that she didn't flirt with audiences in that shameful way that many actresses do," Uhry told the *New York Times*. "I knew that she wouldn't be sentimental or wouldn't be afraid to be mean and nasty. She had always played parts where she wasn't afraid to have the audience not like the character or not think the character was adorable. I could tell that she was an honest actress, as opposed to those TV or movie people who don't play the part, but play themselves."

To his surprise, watching his words played out on stage by Dana Ivey as Daisy gave the playwright new insight into his own life. "Dana has helped me see how really vulnerable this lady is, how you can't be that tight and that unbending without being susceptible underneath. She makes me see a lot that I didn't see as a boy. These are not sentimental people. These are not people who say, *I love you*, even to their own children. But Dana has enabled me to see, for the first time, how much feeling was really there that wasn't being demonstrated."

Ivey admitted to theater reviewer David Kaufman that "sometimes it's obvious that the audience doesn't really like her at first. It takes them a while to begin to warm up to her, just as it took me a while to, because the way she expresses herself is not necessarily the way she feels. She has a great deal of fear and she's masking a lot of that. It's a process of getting to know who she really is aside from the way she presents herself. Much of this happened for me in front of an audience. Their perceptions and their responses taught me things about Daisy that I wasn't aware of myself."

The premise of the play is disarmingly simple. Set in Atlanta, a prickly seventy-two-year-old widow is forced by her son, Boolie, to hire a chauffeur after totaling her car. She has nothing against having a black driver—she resents having to have *anyone* drive her. But Boolie insists and sixty-year-old Hoke comes into her life.

Because the play is basically a two-person drama, the chemistry between Miss Daisy and Hoke is essential. With Ivey hailing from Atlanta and Freeman from Mississippi, the two had an immediate cultural connection and shorthand that resonated through their characters.

"She is a prickly old cactus. But Hoke is no fool, even if he can't read and hasn't seen much of the world," wrote David Richards in his *Washington Post* review.

Gentle without being subservient, he fortifies himself with patience, understanding and the occasional sly witticism, which he tends to mumble under his breath. In Morgan Freeman's sublime performance, the character emerges as a natural aristocrat, who just happened to be born on the wrong side of the tracks.

Before long, the walls between the two begin to crack, and, while they never come tumbling down, a relationship is born through the interstices. Nothing momentous is spoken; both are creatures of few words—her, pointed; his, careful—but the play's subtext is as rich as the Comstock Lode. In the end, when Miss Daisy, teetering on the edge of senility, manages to rally her spirits and admit tearfully, "Hoke, you're my best friend," the humble confession lodges deep in your heart.

Inevitably, the play conjures the myth of the gentile, pre–Civil Rights Movement Old South, a romanticized memory that stubbornly lived on—to Freeman's surprise—in the hearts of many white southerners, who "flocked backstage, bawling and talking about how they're from the South and how it reminds them of family. After a while you start thinking, *Am I evoking nostalgia?* You know? Because this does evoke a time when everybody was sure who they were and what their place was in life. And now things are a little more complicated. So I'd ask my black friends: '*What do you think? What do you feel?*' And they felt the same, that it was a wonderful relationship between two people. They'd say, '*My grandfather was just like that,* or '*It reminds me so much of my uncle.*' So I didn't worry about it."

Seattle Times theater critic Wayne Johnson called the play,

Pure theatrical gold: a funny, charming, affecting miniature that is, in this city of ersatz and hokum, the Real Thing. Only 80 nonstop minutes long, "Driving Miss Daisy" is a quiet play that fairly glows with human decency and honesty, qualities rarely sought, and even more rarely achieved, in the commercial theater here. Potentially touchy matters are handled directly and deftly, usually with humor. . . . Uhry tapped into an autobiographical mother lode, and he mined it with a clear mind, a developed craft and a warm heart. . . .

Dana Ivey, a favorite of dedicated New York playgoers, has been extravagantly praised for her virtuosic portrayal of Miss Daisy, who convincingly ages 25 years in 80 minutes. She deserves all the accolades, but no less important to the production's success is Morgan Freeman's warm and utterly believable performance as Hoke. . . .

An actor friend here told me that every actor in town is dying to get cast in the inevitable movie version of "Driving Miss Daisy."

Driving Miss Daisy, along with *Street Smart*, racking up the acting accolades for Freeman, caused the *New York Times* to track down Freeman for an interview—a sure sign his fortunes were changing. When the reporter commented on the startling difference between Fast Black and Hoke, Freeman remained humble. "You know, changing roles is like stepping over a crack. It's not how wide it is; it's how deep it is. An impressionist can change character instantly by turning away and then turning back to the audience. If you fall into the crack, however."

When it was announced in late 1987 and early 1988, respectively, that he had been nominated for a Golden Globe and an Academy Award, Freeman knew his life had irrevocably changed. "You talk about great timing. It's like God said, *I'm gon't treat this boy right, finally.*"

That it had all come together in 1987 was entirely fitting to Freeman's superstitions. "Every tenth year of my life, every birth year, is when things seemed to click into place for me, and '87 was when I really noticed it. That was when I understood I wasn't going to perish, that I would prevail. '87 was a jump ball, and I was ready. I wasn't gonna kill myself, I wasn't gonna overindulge in drugs or liquor or anything like that."

He was also old enough to stay grounded and to keep perspective in the face of so much praise. "The press come around and tell you that you're just the greatest thing since smoked sausage. You fill out your chest and walk around balancing your head as best you can. But none of that translates into something you can give your landlord or your grocer or your cleaner."

His raised profile also meant that Freeman wouldn't be forced to take any more television roles just to pay the bills. "Everything that's done for television has to be done in a hurry," he says, explaining his reservations about working for the small screen. "If you watch a television movie and watch the actors closely, you can find the first takes because they're just saying the words. If it took six weeks to shoot, you can see the difference between the first week and the last week, where the actor is finally into character after learning him as they go. It's just money. It has nothing to do with work."

Determined to mix it up— "I really don't want to get stuck playing myself"—Freeman's next role was a reformed addict-turned counselor in the 1988 release *Clean and Sober*. In some inspired casting, the film starred Michael Keaton, up to then best known as *Beetlejuice*, who recalls the movie filmed right before Freeman's perfect storm of *Street Smart* and *Driving Miss Daisy* hit.

> We all loved Morgan. He hadn't popped yet and I felt like he was just the coolest guy. Likable, friendly, and told the greatest stories.
>
> One day, we were shooting a scene with a room full of people. And everybody's hanging out, having fun. All of a sudden, Morgan starts screaming. And I'm thinking, *Oh, man. He's crazy.*
>
> And Morgan walks to a corner. I wander over—right?—to ask him: *"What was that all about?"* And Morgan smiles and says, *"They were taking it too easy."* He was right, too. His instincts are so good.

In the film, Keaton plays Daryl, an all-about-me yuppie real estate broker whose penchant for booze, cocaine, and "borrowing" from escrow accounts culminates in him waking up one morning with a dead overdosed blonde in bed beside him and bad investments leaving him owing $50,000 to the escrow account. To buy time, and keep the cops away, he checks into a rehab center—not because he has a problem, mind you, but just for a breather to plan his next moves.

The movie reunited Freeman with his *Street Smart* costar Kathy Baker. This time instead of playing pimp to her whore, he is counselor to her addict.

I enjoyed that experience. I had played a junkie, once, in a TV movie, actually but I didn't really know. But I had a friend who was a counselor. I would try anything, except some things. I would not try heroin just to find out what the high was like. I was scared to death to do that. I would go to my friend and say, *"All right now, tell me this. What happens when you first shoot up, when that jolt hits you— —what's the first thing that happens?"* And he said, *"That's where the nod is. It depends on how much you get as to how deep the nod is and as it wears off you start to get antsier and antsier and antsier; waiting, how are you going to get the next hit."* So I knew what I was doing in terms of playing the character. I also knew where to address it from in terms of the counselor—that sort of no-mercy attitude that you have to have because no one is going to kick the habit for you. You're going to do it, or you're not going to do it. Plain and simple.

In her *New York Times* review, Janet Maslin wrote, "As Craig, Mr. Freeman presides over the group in a wise, watchful manner that gives the entire film extra weight. Without saying much, he seems to understand precisely what each of his charges is going through, and his power to eject them from the center for bad faith or bad behavior becomes daunting to all. The group scenes led by Craig are involvingly staged."

The Washington Post's Rita Kempley added, "Craig, a former addict himself, makes a special project of his most recalcitrant patient. . . . Not a team player, Daryl is surly in group therapy and won't do his push-ups. But when he belittles Craig for his plastic shoes, his nursemaid's job and his $300 salary, he's cheap goods opposite the other man's dignity. Freeman gives a contemplative, instinctive performance here. He's like a nappy-headed Buddha, as serene as his pimp was brutal."

A large part of the film's strength was it avoided clichés—there would be no happy ending, just loss for some and a possible beginning for others.

"It's sophisticated enough to give us more than a simplistic treatment story, conversant enough with its subject to give us the layers of experience that convincingly collide at a treatment center," wrote *Boston Globe*'s Jay Carr. "It's also astute enough to use the fact that the detox and treatment process is a kind of theater, a psychodrama. The emotions of the people undergoing treatment are heightened in ways that go beyond the throes of cold turkey. . . . They're all tightly strung, self-dramatizing, unguided missiles."

The film, directed by *Moonlighting* creator Glenn Gordon Caron, touched on topics a little close to home for Freeman, who openly admitted in publicity junkets he had overcome his own battles with drugs and alcohol.

"I discovered cocaine in the early '80s, when I started making movies. I stopped. I'm not a kid. I've got lots more control over myself."

Although it wasn't an experience he cared to repeat, it had undeniably helped shape him. "I had to go through that to get to here. There is no way to go back and redo that, to say if this hadn't happened, or that hadn't happened."

By the time *Clean and Sober* was released in the summer of 1988, enough time had passed that he was able to reflect on his newfound fame with the self-awareness of someone who had lived more than half a century.

"I am the same person I always was. There's just a lot more water under the bridge now. I guess I have always fantasized. I have always dreamed big dreams. I wasn't always sure they would come true. People say: *'Well Morgan, you finally made it.'* But I made it when I first trod the boards. That was when I could say, *'Mom, look where I am!'*"

Suddenly, Freeman was being inundated with scripts. Unfortunately, few grabbed his attention or interest because "many of them were based on a character I'd already done."

His biggest coup was being cast to reprise Hoke in the feature film being directed by Bruce Beresford and starring Jessica Tandy as Miss Daisy. Initially, though, Beresford seemed to have his doubts about Freeman, which he voiced backstage after coming to see the play.

Freeman recounts the conversation:

"You're a bit young."
"What do you mean I'm a bit young?"
"I mean you're a bit young."
"Did you believe me when you were out there?"
"Yeah, I believed you."
"So what's the problem?"
"You're a bit young."

In retrospect, Beresford's concerns about Freeman's adaptability on screen seemed outrageously misplaced, as with each succeeding role he slipped the characters on with the ease of donning a new coat.

In *Lean on Me,* Freeman tackled the challenge of playing a character based on a living person—a living person who wasn't shy about showing up on the set. The film was a dramatic rendering of Principal Joe Clark's efforts to clean up Eastside High School in Patterson, New Jersey.

Clark had always been a controversial figure—a stickler for discipline who felt righteous in breaking rules he felt were ineffective. His mandate was more boot camp than academic renaissance. Nobody disputes that Eastside High was a school ravaged by drugs, hopelessness, and fear. It was an educational institution basically in name only—a paltry percentage of students were able to pass the state's required basic-skills test, which reflected as badly on the city's politicians as it did school administrators. Although Clark was hired to improve test scores, he felt the only way to do that was to drastically change the environment and the best way to do that was through hard-nosed discipline.

Lean on Me was Freeman's first starring role, and he carried the film with an intensity that matched the real-life Clark's persona. Freeman admits, though, it was not completely comfortable initially knowing the real person was watching.

It started out as an odd and difficult experience—not because Joe was not helpful or anything, it's just that he was there. I have my own voice, my own set of rhythms, and although I studied Joe—followed him around, watched him in action—still I'm dealing with a script and a set parameter and he's himself. When you hear him over the PA system, see how he does things and hear how he uses words, you absorb that. But after a while you pass that . . . it's just a matter of realizing what your limitations are and why.

This observation was somewhat ironic considering Clark wasn't someone who saw himself as having many limitations. *New York Times* reviewer Janet Maslin pokes subtle jabs at Clark and in the same breath she praises Freeman.

It isn't easy to give a good performance while hollering through a bullhorn, but it can be done. And Morgan Freeman manages it in *Lean on Me*. Mr. Freeman marches through the film at full blast, berating the students of Eastside High School in the tough, bombastic style for which Mr. Clark became well known. . . .

He browbeats his staff, he wields a baseball bat, he padlocks school doors in violation of fire laws (to keep out drug dealers) and he insists that all Eastside students be ready to sing the school alma mater on demand. . . .

Audiences are apt to root for the film's Mr. Clark even when they aren't entirely enthusiastic about what he's doing. Much of this is attributable to Mr. Freeman's fiery and compelling performance, but a lot of it also comes from the director John G. Avildsen ("Rocky"), who has stacked the deck in every way he can.

Fortunately, Mr. Freeman . . . humanizes Joe Clark even when the film works overtime to make him larger than life.

The film was number one at the box office for two weeks, solidifying

Freeman's status as both a leading man and an audience draw. For Joe Clark, however, it was a case of being a victim of his own success.

While he was in Los Angeles promoting the film, an assembly he had organized was held for the Eastside Juniors and Seniors. One of the acts was a female singer dressed in a scanty loin cloth and four male dancers dressed in G-strings and a smile. Two stunned vice principals stopped the show and dropped the curtain to the disappointment of the appreciative students.

That in itself would have probably blown over, but when Clark returned, he defended the seminude performance and suspended the two administrators. The Patterson City Council was apoplectic. Despite the fact they had no control over the school board, they drafted a resolution demanding Clark be fired.

Before he could be suspended, Clark announced he would suspend himself for a week—with pay. The superintendent of schools, Frank Napier Jr., a long-time staunch Clark supporter, sadly observed, "The show was more symbolic of something else—that Mr. Clark wasn't paying attention."

Mayor Frank X. Graves Jr., another supporter, was more blunt. "Joe Clark started to get involved in a movie about himself and from that point on, we've had a different Joe Clark. He started, frankly, to get carried away with his own self-unimportance. He seems to have forgotten his commitment to what his job was.

"Joe Clark built a foundation. But the foundation is crumbling and eroding. I say, *Get back with us, Joe. Be one of us.*"

But Clark had other ideas. In a March 1989 *People* interview, he mused, "Maybe in June, I will take some kind of action as far as permanently or temporarily terminating this experience. At the end of this school year, I could be out of here. I could be rewarded commensurately with the expectations of my toils. I could hit the lecture circuit and make five times what I'm making now. I'm a private person. But I'm great on TV. And I think, privately, honestly, that maybe I've outgrown the job anyway." Plus, he added, "I just don't want to put up with the crap."

Clark was coming under increasing criticism in part because the film ended with Freeman as Clark announcing that 75 percent of the students had passed the basic-skills test, thereby stopping a planned takeover of the school by the state. In reality, the scores remained abysmal. Only 30.9 percent of Eastside students passed, compared with an urban average of 57.4 percent and the state's 76.7 percent average.

Clark responded with venom.

This is nothing more than a toxic cynicism perpetrated by jealous, invidious, insidious, surreptitious sapsuckers. But my charge is to not let them dilute my vigor and vim but to fight on. Although they have tried with greatest assiduity to render me impotent, my spirit lingers on.

I see a system that perpetuates inferiority in the inner cities. With inadequate teachers, inadequate supplies, inadequate leadership. I see black and Hispanic youth being exploited. I see now that I'm helpless in raising the educational standards to a reasonable degree at Eastside or anywhere in an inner city. And that tells me, *Joe Clark, maybe you don't want to be part of the destructive mechanism.*

I have national things that I'm dealing with now. I can't stay here because, although I've captured the minds of the nation, I need more. It's like a big fish outgrowing the fishbowl. I've outgrown this.

He added that should he leave Eastside, he hoped that "the damn place blows to smithereens."

For his part, Freeman refused to get caught in the crosshairs of the latest controversies, keeping his focus on the movie and the circumstances that provide the crux of the film.

I spent a lot of time with Joe, discussing this, that and the other, cabbages and kings, as it were . . . I didn't really try to check on the authenticity of events. That was the scriptwriter's job. But I did ask Joe about his emotional state at different times during the controversy. You have to find a way to lock into a person you're playing, warts and all, when that person is a real-life figure.

So I did ask him how bad things at the school really were, at their worst. He said that however bad we make it, it won't be bad enough. He remembers when a group of kids came in one day and turned a pit bull on one of the teachers. Drug use and sale was out in the open. The kids were storing it in their lockers.

He really got into trouble when he chained the school doors during regular hours [to keep out drug-dealing nonstudents]. He took the job with the proviso that he have a free hand, that he not be punished for his actions. But some of what he did outraged a lot of people. He attacked the teachers the same way he attacked everybody else.

When I was in school myself, I came to work, not to play. And there were those teachers who somehow made you think, made you work, made it interesting. I played that, trying to muster as much of that fiery Joe Clark energy as I could.

The postscript of Joe Clark seems to be a cautionary tale of never taking one's press too seriously—something Freeman might have suggested. In the end, Clark did leave Eastside. He eventually landed at the Essex County Juvenile Detention Center in New Jersey, hired to bring order. In 1999, a lawsuit was filed by seven workers who claimed Clark abused children in the center and used his authority to silence potential whistle-blowers. In April 2002, a jury awarded the lead plaintiff $80,000 and a second plaintiff $10,000.

Looking back, Freeman makes it clear he thinks Joe Clark was the victim of misperception. "In movies, you have to simplify to a certain extent, but Joe Clark wasn't simple. Every time he was described, it was as that bullhorn-and-bat-wielding principal. Well, that's total misrepresentation. He wasn't an intimidating man at all in terms of his children. He thought of his children as being victims of the social system. Joe was pissed, but he never took it out on the kids."

Freeman's biggest problem, on the other hand, was deciding which scripts to accept. While other black actors complained about the dearth of roles for people of color, Freeman seemed to transcend race, often getting cast in roles not specifically written for a black man. "Getting jobs is only a problem if you make it a problem. I think some black actors use that as an excuse to whine. I've played Shakespearean roles that weren't written for a black actor, but I was hired. I've often been hired when I'm best for the role."

He refuses to take it personally.

You go to movies and it's science fiction and it's in the future, the bomb has gone off, and here are the survivors. And they're all white. No blacks, no Chinese, no Indians, no Hispanics. So as you get older, you understand.

I imagine that if I wrote, I would write about black people, so there's no reason to hold a pistol to a white writer's head and say, *"Write about black people."* They write about what they know about, it's as simple as that, and after a while you realize you can't beat your head against the wall because you're attacking people for the wrong reasons. It's not white writers' responsibility. You want material, write it.

Despite the nonstop film work, part of Freeman's heart still belonged to the theater and its special allure. "That instant gratification. And actors are always concerned with power, that megalomaniac control of an entire room. In film, the writer and director and editor all have final say. But in the theater, once that curtain goes up, it's all up to the actors. Nothing gets said unless you say it."

But until the next stage role came along, he was quite content to say it on film.

5

THERE ARE SOME film roles that go beyond interesting characters or good paydays; some matter. For Morgan Freeman, *Glory* was one of those projects. It wasn't so much that the film boasted a bevy of talented black actors, including Denzel Washington and Andre Braugher, as it was the men these actors portrayed—the soldiers of the Fifty-fourth Massachusetts Regiment of Volunteer Infantry, America's first black combat regiment.

Organized in March 1863 by abolitionists, the regiment was under the command of twenty-six-year-old Colonel Robert Gould Shaw. Most of the recruits were free blacks from the north, including the two sons of noted abolitionist Frederick Douglass.

According to *New York Times* writer Richard Bernstein, "Douglass believed that blacks should be involved in a fight that was, at least in part, for their own freedom. Abolitionists, like John Albion Andrew, governor of Massachusetts, believed that the regiment would be a step toward a wider acceptance of blacks by whites, a proof of their claim on full citizenship in the America of just a few months after the Emancipation Proclamation."

On July 18, the regiment engaged Confederate soldiers at Fort Wagner, suffering severe losses—nearly half the soldiers were killed, including Colonel Shaw. But their valiant fighting became legendary and helped spur an onslaught of black enlistment. A year later, the Fifty-fourth was dispatched to Florida and provided important backup to other Union troops as the rearguard. For the rest of the war, the regiment fought throughout the South until it was formally disbanded in August 1865. Although there was never any dispute about the importance of the Fifty-fourth's contributions among historians, their exploits were not usually extolled in American schools and were largely forgotten.

The movie *Glory* changed that.

One of Morgan Freeman's vivid memories as a kid was the lack of black screen heroes. And the few black characters he did see were little more than stereotypes. "I didn't know anybody who acted like that."

Glory, on the other hand, was replete with fully fleshed roles that told an important fact-inspired story about the contribution of black soldiers—although it didn't necessarily start that way.

Freeman says he was asked to work on the project by producer Freddie Fields and director Ed Zwick. "And so we put this movie together and we went to Savannah, Georgia, and for three weeks we rehearsed it and we wrote it. It was framed around a war without fleshed-out characters. We had character skeletons—so each actor got to actually put the meat on the bones of his character and it was a great experience. You see a lot of stuff in *Glory* that we actually sat down and improvised and then wrote down."

Freeman played John Rawlins, an illiterate grave digger who rises through the ranks to make sergeant major. It was a role especially close to the actor's heart.

I have a special affinity for seeing to it that our history is told. The Black legacy is as noble, is as heroic, is as filled with adventure and conquest and discovery as anybody else's. It's just that nobody knows it.

I read history as a hobby because I'm interested in my own. It's important to know so you have a sense of yourself. In a place of your own. Nobody can give you a sense of place.

For as much as Freeman loved the process of acting, performance became something special when coupled with history.

"You go along, and you work and you work and you work and you work, and people say, *Oh, you do good work, great movies, blah, blah, blah.* And then something comes along that just defines your whole *raison d'être*, your reason for being. *Glory* was that for me.

"It's one of the most important things I've done," he says. "I think it's one of the most important things *anybody* has done. Everybody involved in it, I think, was very spiritually involved. This is a moment in history that had been excised, forgotten about; to bring that back where it belongs, close to the heart, is a wonderful undertaking.

"*Glory* . . . had something to teach. It told people something they didn't know. It was almost a documentary in its adherence to truth."

The film became a labor of love and was critically acclaimed. Jay Carr in *The Boston Globe* was effusive.

Nowhere on Hollywood's long list of war movies is there anything like *Glory*. Simply put, it's the most overdue war movie ever made, filled with terrible beauty, richness and grandeur. It's more accurate than all but a few, not only reflecting American history, but putting right its glaring downplaying of the pivotal role of black troops fighting on the Union side in the Civil War. . . .

As few American films of any genre do, it musters epic sweep, dignity and conviction. . . . *Glory* builds slowly, never lapsing into false heroics, giving the real heroism of the black soldiers a chance to move us. And it does, with a tender, tragic force you seldom encounter at the movies.

Although Colonel Shaw was a historical figure, Freeman's Rawlins was a fictional composite, meaning Morgan had to create his own backstory. "I studied slave narratives and pored over photographs and daguerreotypes," Freeman says. "The first thing I decided was not to look too clean, too store-bought. We decided he came from Virginia. One of the things Virginia was famous for was breeding farms. They didn't care at all for families. Rawlins had family, we decided, but they were sold out from under him."

In Freeman's view, Rawlins is the glue that holds the regiment together because he acts as a bridge between the white leaders and the black grunt soldiers. "He was the connecting point. We first see him as a grave digger at Antietam. Having buried so many boys—shards shreds, pieces of people—I'm sure he had a rather morbid perspective. But it also gave him a sense of the responsibility they were undertaking. For any black man, that was one of the most important events in the history of our country. It was going to mean taking off the shackles. There was no way not to take part in that battle."

Unlike the war movies Freeman grew up watching that downplayed the human cost to promote patriotism, *Glory* showed that fighting for one's beliefs always exacts a huge individual cost.

New York Times reviewer Vincent Canby said,

> The attack on Fort Wagner, which is the climax of the movie, comes as close to anything I've ever seen on screen to capturing the chaos and brutality that were particular to the Civil War battles. Weapons maimed as often as they killed. Soldiers were so disciplined that they marched in firm lines into the sights of guns fired at point-blank range. Hand-to-hand combat was commonplace.
>
> The toll taken in each battle was, of course, enormous. Yet still the men continued to move forward. They had to believe in what they were doing. For all of the carnage and suffering, the Civil War was a time of limitless optimism for many, something that now seems immensely sad. *Glory* is celebratory, but it celebrates in a manner that insists on acknowledging the sorrow.

Richard Bernstein agreed.

> In *Glory* war is clearly hell. The battle scenes of this movie seem graphically true to a historical reality, reflected in a simple statistic. Some 700,000 soldiers died in the Civil War, more than half the total number of deaths, 1.2 million, suffered in all of the wars of the United States combined. Half a dozen or so major battles during the Civil War produced casualty rates in the vicinity of 20 percent, a massacre by today's standards. Nonetheless, the battlefield in *Glory* is presented as an arena wherein individual men come to have respect for one another. War is a place of ultimate questions and ultimate confrontations that both destroy men and forge brotherhood among them.

Freeman wasn't the only actor who felt passionate about the film—every actor took a significant pay cut to participate. But for Morgan the real payoff had nothing to so with cash.

"This is the kind of picture that gives legitimacy to the history of people of color, and tells us who we are. Black men have fought and died in every conflict this nation was involved in, from the Revolutionary War onward. We are Americans, and we fought and died to be Americans. I hope the film will go a long way towards raising people's awareness."

Denzel Washington, who would win the Best Supporting Actor Academy Award for his portrayal of Trip, a former slave, added, "Freedom was not given to us in some paternalistic way; it was something we had to claim with blood. Well, they never taught me that in my school."

Perhaps not so coincidentally, around this time Freeman began developing a new appreciation of his southern heritage. Even though he had lived in New York almost half his life, it had never really become his home. Starting in the early 1980s, he had begun visiting Mississippi regularly, partly to visit his parents but mostly he found himself drawn by some primal siren's song.

His youngest daughter Morgana, however, was less than thrilled with her father's search for his roots. "I was a city girl, and there was nothing to do down there. I was scared of the horses, and I did not like to see my food get killed."

But Colley-Lee fell in love with Mississippi, which is one reason they had decided to get married at his parents' home. "I was shaped and molded by the South, and I never got Northernized. I realized I was a Southerner because every time I went back home, I'd slip into it very comfortably. I like it there. It's home."

Realizing he was successful enough to live anywhere he chose, Freeman returned to Mississippi permanently, settling in Charleston. In addition to the forty-four acres owned by his parents, Morgan and Myrna bought an additional eighty acres on which they eventually built a house. They now live on land Morgan's family and ancestors worked on as slaves.

The mea culpa of the prodigal southern son coming home isn't lost on Freeman.

I swore I'd never come back to live. I didn't care what happened to this state. I thought it was one of the most backward places on Earth. But then my parents came back in the midfifties . . . and as I started to grow up, seeing what the world was like and then coming back here to visit, I started seeing with grown-up eyes.

It all finally goes back to my great-great-great-grandmother who was brought here from Virginia, pretty much that extended family, all from Mississippi, and you look at it like that and think, *Why should I give up my whole history?* Gradually it began to dawn on me that I didn't do too badly growing up here, that my life here wasn't so traumatic.

Growing up in Mississippi, I realized that it was separate and unequal and all that, but it was still a safe place to be—I spent enough time growing up in Chicago to make a qualitative comparison between growing up in an urban jungle and growing up in a village. And believe me, the village is better.

Like many who grow up in rural areas, the inherent lifestyle of metropolitan living began to wear thin on Freeman. "It's a certain attitude about life and other people. You're walking down the street, you don't know the next person, but they say hello. Living in a small town, I have neighbors. I lived twenty-five years in New York, and for most of it, I didn't even know who was in the next apartment, I didn't care, I didn't even want to know. Your humanity starts to suffer as a result."

Of course, small town life is much nicer when money isn't an issue. And he's honest enough to admit that being famous certainly helped roll out an especially warm welcome mat. "When I moved home, all my neighbors, none of whom at the time were black, all came to say welcome. . . . My immediate neighbor grinned at me one day and said, '*I'm sure glad you moved here; our property values went up.*' Ironic, isn't it?"

6

MORGAN FREEMAN DOESN'T merely portray his characters; he seamlessly and fluidly *inhabits* them. Fast Black and Rawlins and Zeke stuck in the minds of the audience because they had a true human depth. It's ironic then how Freeman refuses to mystify his process.

"My understanding of acting is that it's pretending. Some think it's something other than pretending, but it isn't. That's what I've been doing since I was a child. . . . A lot of people get into the acting game and if they make it early, it loses its importance to their lives. Maybe they think it's not a worthy occupation for an adult. So they have to give it much more importance than it really has."

He goes so far as to suggest acting isn't a true art form.

"Art is a person confronting a blank page or an empty canvas. With acting, it's handed to you. The purest form of acting would be without costumes or sets. But they give you a complete script and have all this believability built around you. You're not creating anything. You're just channeling. What's great about it, of course, is that in both movies and onstage, but particularly in movies, you've got an army of people all hauling in the same direction. It's great fun."

But propping up all this pretending is a big money business. And without financing, there is no fun. Despite being a stage hit and an obvious project to turn into a film, many in Hollywood believe *Driving Miss Daisy* only made it to screen thanks to the passionate efforts of producer Jake Eberts.

The saga began when Lily and Richard Zanuck bought the rights to Alfred Uhry's play in 1987. To their surprise, the reaction from the studios was decidedly cool, even after the play won a Pulitzer. Zanuck, whose father Darryl founded 20th Century Fox Studios, was stunned.

"Everywhere we went, we heard the same thing: '*Look, it's going to be a wonderful picture and maybe win an award or two. But who's going to go see it?*' One studio executive asked us, '*Are you locked into that cast? Maybe we could put someone with more marquee in there. Hey, what about Eddie Murphy?*'"

Determined to have the cast they wanted, they reworked the budget and trimmed it down to an almost anorexic $7.5 million and made the rounds again.

Still no takers.

The rejections took their toll, and the Zanucks came close to moving on. "At one point, I turned to Lili. '*This is embarrassing,*' I said," Richard told the *New York Times*. "*I've been in this business all my life, and now we're being turned down by people I've never even heard of!*"

Eventually, Warner Brothers expressed interest, but was only willing to finance part of the budget.

In walked Jake Eberts.

Canadian-born, London-based Eberts began his producing career by helping finance *Watership Down*, the 1978 animated film adaptation of Richard Adam's fantasy book about a group of rabbits looking for a new home. Over the next dozen years, he produced films including *Chariots of Fire, Gandhi, Hope and Glory, Last Exit to Brooklyn*, and *Dances with Wolves* which won a collective fifteen Oscars.

At one point he had inquired into the rights of *Driving Miss Daisy*, which the Zanucks had already acquired. To the Zanucks' relief, Eberts shared their passion for the project. "Jake didn't seem to have any hesitation," Mr. Zanuck told Paul Chutkow in a 1990 interview. "He read the script, and afterward he called and said, '*I like it, I like the material, I like the cast, and you've been faithful to the material.*' The decision-making process moved very quickly."

Eberts ponied up $3.25 million in exchange for the film's foreign rights on top of Warner Brothers' kicked in $4.5 million.

Whatever reservations director Bruce Beresford might have had about Freeman being too young to play Miss Daisy's chauffer Hoke Colburn evaporated once the filming began. Later, Beresford would be one of the converted, enthusing, "I think Morgan could do almost anything. I think he and Robert Duvall are the two most skillful actors I have ever worked with in my life. Technically, they have enormous resources."

In the years since he originated the role Off-Broadway, Freeman had occasion to see other actors play Hoke—experiences that left the actor ever-so-slightly territorial.

"It turned me off. Some actors played him really angry. Some played him with his hat in his hand, really deferential. It's a tricky character, right on the edge of Uncle Remus. But I knew how to play him right away. I knew when I read it. I just saw him—the dignity in the character. The thing about Hoke is that he has this ironclad dignity. However you choose to play him, you must first cloak him in this dignity."

The playwright was aware that his material needed a deft hand. "A movie like this could easily be oversentimental," he told writer Myra Forsberg.

So I made it clear I wanted to write the screenplay, and nobody seemed to mind that, which I found surprising because I had never written one.

Miss Daisy was so ingrained in me as a play that the original line readings were in my ears. So I had to think, *If I were going to a movie about this, what do I want to see?* Bruce kept saying, "*If you can show me what they're talking about, show it.*" There were a lot of scenes in the play where we talked about things that happened, and I found in almost every case I could do that. The problem, though, was this is a culture where storytelling is important, and I didn't want all the stories shown. So there's still some, *I remember the time that so and so did this* in it, because that's very Southern.

I know enough about the movies to realize that verisimilitude can't hurt. The core relationship was what was important. I wanted to preserve what I'd written: an honest representation of the South the way I remembered it.

Freeman says the character he developed was a composite of several people, including his own father who worked as a chauffeur when the family lived in Nashville. "My father worked as a domestic when he was much younger for a lady that was crazy about him. I think that will happen," particularly with women who are left with a large house to run after their husband dies. "And they hire someone to take care of it, and when they come in and start taking care of it, they're taking care of you. And the irony, the beauty of this piece is they get this real close relationship and yet they keep that distance.

"It's the servant-employer relationship. That's going to continue no matter what. It reflects the way that our society is stratified, black and white. And these are not young people—they're not going to change their way of looking at things. But still these relationships develop . . . there's something that they can depend on in the framework."

Even so, Freeman was aware that some people characterized Hoke as an Uncle Tom.

"People who don't know the South are fast to judge it, like they do Hoke. He kept his head up under that cap he wore. I based a lot of Hoke on my father. Guys like him were pretty sly, and spoke a different language around white people. Maybe it's why I was so happy it got the attention. All of those people like that, I knew them very well."

New York Times reviewer Rosellen Brown noted that the movie's social commentary is subtly couched within what is essentially a two-character study.

The movie version of Alfred Uhry's play *Driving Miss Daisy* is, of course, not meant to be about such abstractions as civil rights or bigotry. . . . The charm of *Miss Daisy* challenges no one; it goes down easy as Key lime pie. The movie turns out to be about friendship, about dignity and aging, but it plays teasingly, almost always by indirection, with the very unlikeliness of the nearly forbidden alliance of two humans of different colors breaking through to each other's deeper needs. . . .

Paradoxically the movie hints (but would never say) that although we follow Hoke and Miss Daisy up to 1973, had their friendship begun in the mid-60's in a time of racial turmoil, let alone today, this individual triumph of affection over status could never have taken place. When a man like Hoke stops being ingratiating (and flawless in every detail of his performance of duty), such friendships are doomed.

Not surprisingly, the film prompted discussions about New South versus Old South and the state of race relations in this country and whether anything was really any better. Freeman spoke openly about his own experiences with prejudice early in his career. "I had those viciously sad and discouraging—distraught—moments when I thought, *There's no place in this world for me. How am I gonna get along?* But I tried to always think about the next step in the evolution, because that's the cheap out. You can fall back on that one. You gotta want it, and you gotta keep at it."

Freeman credits his mother and others who encouraged his talent with helping strengthen that inner resolve.

I remember my mother giving me the impression I was special when I was growing up. And then my teachers gave me the impression I was special. And then the townsfolk gave me the feeling I was special. And I get out here into the world and think, *I'm special.*

If you keep plugging away, things can bear out. It wasn't like

I was a big fish in a dry pond—it gave me the encouragement to do what I had to in this business. My mother made me feel like I was a star growing up, and I remember the first time I was in Los Angeles in the late '50s, standing on Sunset Boulevard, thinking I was gonna prove her right. It took a while, though.

For the movie, director Beresford was adamant to have an actress of a certain age for Daisy. "A lot of actresses who wanted to play it were in their late 40's and early 50's, and I said in the first place we're going to have a nightmare with the makeup and in the second place I think it'll be slightly absurd," he explained to the *New York Times*. "I had this vision of myself making this film with some young woman doddering around and every critic in the world saying, *Bruce is a fool*. I'm just relieved we got Jessica Tandy."

Tandy, then eighty, replaced Dana Ivey, who in her later forties was too young for the role. Tandy empathized with Ivey. Tandy originated the role of Blanche DuBois in Tennessee Williams's *Streetcar Named Desire* but was passed over in favor of Vivian Leigh for the film—the only cast member of the play not given the chance to reprise their role on screen. Although Tandy worked in almost forty films over the span of her career, it was never in a lead—or bankable—role. Being cast in *Daisy* prompted her to comment that she felt as if she was being rediscovered by filmmakers.

Insurers, though, were nervous about an octogenarian leading lady filming in Georgia during the summer so Tandy was forced to pay for a completion bond out of her own pocket. But the actress considered it a small price to pay in order to to play the character she described to writer Glenn Collins as being admittedly prickly.

"She was the product of her time and she had the prejudices of her time. But she does grow. She learns. By the end of the film she's really changed. And you know, the whole world changed at the time."

Film review Jay Carr observed in the *Boston Globe* that it's the subtlety of that change that informed the movie so powerfully.

One seldom writes about the innate power of decency and goodness because it's hard to do so without turning ridiculous. But the fact is that both Hoke and Miss Daisy radiate enormous strength of character and spirit. There's astonishing richness and emotional impact in the restraint that Tandy and Freeman make the key to their work. In their different ways, each makes every gesture, every instant register. It's a relief that the film can comfortably slip into a languorous Southern pace; it never tries clumsily to load each moment with significance. Yet Tandy and Freeman make even the quiet sections throb with meaning. . . .

Thanks mostly to them, it's one of the few films that actually surpasses the play from which it's drawn. They know just what to do with close-ups and the intimate scale. . . .

Freeman is note-perfect with Hoke's dignified warmth, and Tandy, whose every moment on screen is an acting lesson, turns in what by far is the most hauntingly elegant performance of the year. While Freeman stakes his claim as an American actor second to none, Tandy, at the age of 80, seems to have passed beyond technique into something like pure essence.

The Washington Post heaped on more praise. "The movie gets you mainly because Morgan Freeman, who played chauffeur Hoke Colburn in the original stage production (and won his third Obie for it), takes the wheel and drives *Daisy* all the way home. . . . Freeman has taken whatever black parts Hollywood has thrown his way and transformed them."

Reviewers were outdoing one another with superlatives. Howie Movshovitz in *The Denver Post* rhapsodized,

Morgan Freeman's performance lifts the script gloriously. The role is in Freeman's body, in his gestures and expressions. He acts the servant, but his moves show you his independence. . . .

Beresford lets the camera linger over moments of silence, so that Freeman's pace and look overcome the stagey, clichéd dialogue.

Tandy is her usual sentimental self, which is fine for this part, but Freeman makes the movie click. . . .

You don't see stuff like this often. The quiet dignity of Hoke and Miss Daisy show you what politeness really means, and how manners can be a way to social change. Neither of them is of our time—they seem out of this world—but you wish people could rise above themselves the way these two do.

When all the box office was tallied, *Driving Miss Daisy* grossed more than $145 million worldwide and an additional $fifty million in rentals, off a combined $7.5 million original budget, making it one of the most profitable films of the decade.

Forgive Richard Zanuck if he doesn't indulge in a little bit of *I told you so*. "What *Daisy* proves is that there are millions and millions of people who are hungry for alternative fare from what we've been providing them: the obvious commercial film. There is a very sizable audience out there for movies that are not about sex, car chases, violence or madness."

Eberts told the *New York Times* that it was just another case of studios not knowing their audience.

One observation I could make about European filmmaking is that people tend to make films which they want to make, whereas here in America people seem to make films that they think other people will want to see.

That puts a terrible demand on your objectivity. It forces you to say, *If I was 18 years old, and living in the San Fernando Valley what would I want to go and see?* The Europeans tend to say, *Gee, I love this story. This is a story I'd like to make. It's important to me, and because I feel that way, I'm sure the audience will feel that way, too.*

As a general rule the Europeans would sooner be given a *Legion d'Honneur* pin than make some money, because that really establishes them as a figure in the arts. That is a very big difference between the two cultures.

In the case of *Daisy*, art and commerce were not mutually exclusive. The film and its two stars won Golden Globes in the musical/comedy motion picture categories, the National Board of Review named *Daisy* best picture and Freeman best actor, and Uhry was honored by the Writers' Guild of America. So it came as no surprise when the film earned nine Academy Award nominations, including nods for Tandy, Freeman, and Uhry. The only dent in the celebration was the glaring omission of Bruce Beresford, who was shut out of the best director category.

Leading up to the Oscars, the attention was almost blinding, and most critics had as good as given Freeman the award. But the actor had been around too long to let himself get completely carried away by all the adulation being tossed his way.

"Boy, you've gotta be careful with that kind of talk—I might start walking through thinking, *They're going to like me anyway, so I don't have to work too hard here.* I always explain my life as life itself," he says, "as this cycle, this wheel that continuously moves and has these highs and lows. I think of this year as being just one of those high years. But you can't take your work for granted. You either give it its due or don't do it, it's as simple as that. In a job situation like this, when you've worked and struggled to get where you are, you don't want to pretend it's not important to you."

Uhry, for one, was confident Freeman would handle the attention with his usual aplomb, in large part because Freeman possesses "a deep and abiding sense of humor—especially about the fact that this year, he's hot. He's not about to forget the dark years."

There was additional buzz for the Oscars that year because Denzel Washington had also been nominated for *Glory*, marking the first time two black men had been included in both acting categories in the same year. But it would be a bittersweet night for Freeman.

As expected, Jessica Tandy was named best actress, making her the oldest person ever to win an Academy Award. Uhry won for best adapted screenplay. The movie won best picture. But in an upset, Daniel Day-Lewis won for his role as a quadriplegic in *My Left Foot* over Freeman. His *Glory* costar, Denzel Washington, was named best supporting actor.

Many in Hollywood, especially among the black community, felt Freeman was robbed. It was no secret that the five-thousand-plus then-members of the Academy were primarily white so it was easy to accuse the industry of tacit racism. However, Freeman refused to jump on the bandwagon, maintaining, "It's all about merit."

Lifelong activist Ossie Davis was also benign. "I don't worry about that," he told the *Washington Post*. "I've been doing this a long time, and I'm happy to see what we've created. We have learned to respect our own images, and we've helped the industry appreciate who we are."

The bigger issue was the lack of roles for black actors—and the paucity of black executives in positions of green-lighting, as well as the scarcity of black writers and directors. Robert Johnson, then Black Entertainment Television owner, told writer Sharon Waxman that's why it was imperative for networks like BET to expand their production horizons.

> I think the general view is that there's probably not an artistic bias in the academy, but if you don't send as many African American actors, writers, directors up to bat, the odds of them being selected for the Oscars is obviously less. The only way to change that is for the system to open up the doors to more African American writers. As a result of that you'll get more African American scripts, which would require African American actors. But many of those decisions are business decisions. And those who decide to green-light a film don't believe they can match a great white actor with a great black actress. That's the kind of courage people have to put out.

In a 1990 essay for *Ebony*, Lena Horne lamented the slow advancement of blacks in the industry and agreed with Johnson that blacks rising into executive levels was imperative.

> We have the performing, writing, directing and technical talent to create the whole range of art and entertainment. But all

that talent means nothing without the all-important element of economic power. We need more producers who have the power to make decisions about what gets produced. . . . .

We also have to create and control the business networks that enable us to distribute our product to the largest possible audience, at home and around the world.

Sometimes, change almost goes unnoticed. That summer, Freeman returned to the stage as Petruchio in a Central Park production of *The Taming of the Shrew* opposite Tracey Ullman in a production that was set in the American South. It wasn't so much color-blind casting as it was allowing a great actor a worthy forum. "Morgan's mind is never a blank," says Joseph Papp, "and you see that onstage. It's as if he's had 1,000 years of living experience. But also, he has the good speech required for Shakespeare."

Freeman remembers that production for a more humbling reason. "It was the first time that I froze in front of an audience. I forgot all of my lines and there wasn't anyone there who was able to prompt me. The situation was a bad one and all the other actors on the stage were looking at me with this challenge on their face like *What you gonna do now, fool, to get out of this?*" Freeman swears that to this day he can't remember how he got through the scene.

Maybe it was that experience that led to his epiphany. Although Freeman spent the first two decades of his career primarily as a stage actor, he eventually accepted that his preference was film. "I was on the stage a long time, all the time trying to get into the movies. My whole life has been me aiming to get into the movies." Even so, "For years I told myself I was going back to theater. I did *Taming of the Shrew* in 1990. I was mostly concerned with the idea that it was such hard work. It was really wearing me out. I had done 20 years of theater with the idea of getting into the movies. Now I'm in movies. I don't have to go back to prove something. That was what my life and childhood was all about: the movies."

Never one to micromanage, Freeman didn't worry about where the next job would come from, quite content to enjoy the down time sailing his thirty-eight-foot ketch christened *Sojourner*. His philosophy was that his next role "will choose me. There's a lot of stuff out there, a lot of people writing. I'm just waiting until somebody comes along and says, *Here's a good part*—and has a bucketful of money to do it."

7

AFTER ALL THE years he spent waiting to be recognized and respected as a film actor, Freeman seemed thrown off balance when it finally happened. As soon as the flurry of media attention died down after the Academy Awards, Freeman escaped to the Virgin Island of St. Martin to go sailing on the *Sojourner* and regain his equilibrium.

"He's having a little bit of trouble accepting this success right now," his wife Myrna Colley-Lee admitted to *Ebony* in 1990. "He wants [the success], and he's enjoying it, but it just hasn't set in that it's really happening for him right now."

More specifically, Freeman was having trouble with the concept of being *a star*.

> You're not really successful in this business unless you're famous. So you want to be famous. The problem is, see, I'm a character actor; which means I have a shot at a lot of diverse roles—the sort of characters who are buried inside the story rather than the ones who are carrying the story. When you become a star, it

gets to the point where . . . a lot of the time, they're hiring you because of your face.

I don't particularly care for the *movie star* label. It's like my agent says, and I believe it: Once you become a movie star, people come to see you. You don't have to act anymore. And, to me, that's a danger.

The bigger danger, though, was how producers and directors viewed him. Freeman's biggest fear was being typecast. "I try always to go beyond the image of myself. I don't want do something I've already done. I don't want to be something I've already been. I can't tell you how many street jives I got after *Street Smart*."

His pet peeve is when he receives scripts from screen writers who say, "'*I wrote this with you in mind, this is you.*' No, this *isn't* me. This is some character I've already done. If you wrote it with me in mind, that's your first mistake." Freeman also discovered the fine line that actors need to navigate to avoid pigeonholing. "*Driving Miss Daisy* kind of ruined a lot of things," he admits. "People see you as very loving and dependable and stable, and they want you to be that way because there's really something secure in it for audiences. So I get a lot of the sensitive, caring, doctor, preachers, psychiatrists, whatever."

Even though he maintains, "In acting, you want to be eclectic and move through and do it all," he admits there are limits. "I can't recall a romantic comedy ever having crossed my desk"—which is fine by him. "I don't feel romantic at all on screen. I did a love scene once, and we were making love and it's hard. It's really hard work."

Freeman's next role was a decidedly unromantic role. Based on the mammoth novel by Tom Wolf, *The Bonfire of the Vanities* starred Tom Hanks as Wall Street trader Sherman McCoy whose life is shredded after he leaves the scene of an accident.

When we first meet McCoy in the film he is a self-important millionaire trader who enjoys the trappings of success—his expensive care, his expensive lifestyle, his expensive mistress, Maria, a southern belle gold digger played by Melanie Griffith. One night McCoy and

Maria get lost in the Bronx driving home from the airport. When McCoy realizes he's in the hood, he panics, and in his haste to get out, accidentally runs over a black youth. He leaves the scene and fails to notify police so an honest accident becomes a hit-and-run case that is sniffed out by a down on his luck, booze bleary tabloid reporter named Fallow, brought to smarmy life by Bruce Willis.

McCoy suddenly finds himself the center of a *cause célèbre* with politicians and activists and religious leaders all trying to use the accident to further their own self-serving agendas. Fallow doesn't let facts stand in the way of his story and wins a Pulitzer for his equally misleading spin of the events while McCoy's life disintegrates.

For all the script's intrigue, the story behind the camera was more dramatic than what ended up on screen. During the production New Jersey Supreme Court Justice Robert N. Wilentz banned the film crew from shooting at the county courthouse—costing the county a $250,000 location fee. The scenes in question depicted a protest by a mob of angry black citizens that devolves into a riot after Hank's character is acquitted. Wilentz determined that the movie would give the impression that minorities did not get treated fairly in the courts. His decision angered Essex County Executive Nicholas Amato, who had anticipated using the location fee to pay for much-needed repairs. So Amato sued Wilenz, accusing the jurist of censorship, noting other productions had been previously allowed to film at the Newark courthouse, including *She Devil*, *Presumed Innocent*, and *Jacob's Ladder*.

However, Wilentz's initial ruling was applauded by the citizens of the Bronx and local black leaders, who were furious at the way the book characterized their borough—even though Wolf's opus skewered *everyone*, from greedy Wall Street traders to the courts to journalists to black activists. Still, Bronx residents demanded the filmmakers put a disclaimer on the film—despite nobody having seen it.

Even before all the controversy erupted, the producers made an important character change during preproduction in hopes of preventing charges of racism. The judge in Wolf's book was Myron

Kovitsky—a tough, fair-minded white Jewish man. In the film, he became Morgan Freeman.

"Originally they hired Alan Arkin to play my role," he explains. "I thought that was perfect casting. But then they thought they had to be politically correct and make the judge black. So they fired Alan Arkin and hired me. Not a great way to get a role. I was kind of a suck-ass for not turning it down, but they weren't going to give it back to Alan anyway," despite having to pay his full six-figure salary.

Director Brian DePalma told *New York Times* writer Tim Golden he simply changed his mind. "I didn't want to racially polarize it. I didn't want a white judge talking morality to a basically black audience."

The decision was expensive beyond having to pay off Arkin; Freeman's schedule prevented the courtroom scenes from being filmed in Los Angeles which translated into huge expenses trying to find an available courtroom on the East Coast since the Newark courthouse remained off limits.

Ironically, shortly before the film's release United States District Judge Nicholas H. Politan ruled that Judge Wilentz had in fact violated the Constitution, noting, "He prevented the filming solely based on his objection to what the filmmaker intended to say and the fear that such a viewpoint would reflect poorly upon the judiciary. This is nothing more than an attempt to bolster the reputation of the court by infringing upon the constitutional rights of others."

Although the District Court rejected Amato's request that Wilentz personally pony up the lost $250,000, the judge did warn Wilentz that further such bans on moviemaking may result in imposed fines.

Unfortunately, none of the publicity generated by the ruling did much to help the film, although typically, Freeman escaped unscathed. In his review, Jay Carr of the *Boston Globe* wrote that while none of the actors were given much to work with, "Worst served of all is Morgan Freeman. . . . He's given a pseudo-Capraesque upbeat curtain speech that would cause any actor of less intrinsic dignity and presence to shrivel with embarrassment. The book at least had the brass to convincingly sink its teeth into some of the uglier aspects of New York life

. . . the film condescendingly trivializes the tapestry of social ills the book reflected. De Palma's *Bonfire of the Vanities* . . . rests on the mud of a bad idea that just keeps getting more wrong as it proceeds."

Washington Post reviewer Rita Kempley noted, "Not surprisingly, Freeman offers one of the film's finest performances, though even he can't finesse the clumsy moral coda that advises us: *Go home and be decent.*" She then sniped, "*The Bonfire of the Vanities* has become a much smaller conflagration, a pilot light of the inanities in Brian De Palma's whitewashed screen adaptation. . . . He has not only filed Wolfe's teeth but stuck his tail between his legs. A calamity of miscasting and commercial concessions, this *Bonfire* is fed with twigs. . . .

"In Wolfe's story, all of New York was held accountable, but De Palma and Cristofer seem to blame the woes of the '80s mostly on the press, black rabble-rousers and women. As usual, the white male floats like fat to the top of the melting pot."

Freeman says he knew the movie was doomed. "I don't think Brian De Palma had a clue. It struck me that he didn't read the book—or that he didn't like the book. It was the one time Tom Hanks was awfully miscast. . . . I never did get around to seeing the movie."

By the time *Bonfire* went down in flames, Freeman was immersed in his next roles. First up was a remake of *Robin Hood*, starring Kevin Costner as a rather dour and moody prince of thieves. Freeman's character, a Moor named Azeem who becomes devoted to Robin Hood for saving his life, was created for the film, and the actor was thrilled to inject a little historical accuracy into the part.

"One critic said of *Robin Hood, Well, I don't know if you'd have seen a black man in England in the twelfth century. . . . That sort of sums it up.* He didn't know. Here's a lesson on him."

Coryn Weigle who owns a shop specializing in medieval objects concurred, telling the *Washington Post*, "There was quite a bit of travel during the Crusades; blacks were not totally unknown. At least locals were more likely to see a black man, say, than a dragon."

Tampering with a myth as well known as Robin Hood was made less dicey by taking the leap with Freeman. *Boston Globe* critic Jay Carr noted, "What's most daring about the production is the screenplay. . . . I was about to write that it risks introducing a new character to the legendary band. . . . But since the newcomer . . . is played by Morgan Freeman, the risk is not only minimal, but downright nonexistent. Freeman is a plus in whatever production he happens to show up in."

Rita Kempley agreed, writing in her *Washington Post* review, "Freeman's Azeem is a wonderfully ironic fellow, a cultured Saracen who introduces the telescope, gun powder and the C-section to the quaint tree-dwellers. Verily, they seem less like a band of dispossessed Saxons than a tribe of primitive Ewoks."

While Freeman says every job should be a creative challenge—"The challenge is to do it and make it look right, like you belong there, wherever that is"—he admitted that *Robin Hood* was also physically challenging.

"The thing I remember most is being in pain. We were up in northern England in the winter, and I don't do cold very well. Just prior to going there, my wife had bought me this shiatsu massage in New York, and they stepped on my back and pinched a nerve. And then during filming I jumped off a wall, and my knee went backward. So I remember standing in the mud in the cold with this pain running up my leg and hip. They got me an osteopath to try to work it out. He never could."

The advantage of being an in-demand movie star is that you can afford the luxury of accepting projects that offered smaller paydays but greater potential personal satisfaction. *The Power of One* was one of those films. Based on the semiautobiographical novel by Bryce Courtnay, the story is set in the 1930s and 1940s, following the first eighteen years in the life of British boy, PK, living in South Africa.

PK grows up fatherless, his dad having been killed by an elephant shortly before he was born. The boy is raised by his frail mother and the Zulus who work the family farm. When his mother falls ill and dies, he is sent to a harsh, anti-British boarding school, populated by many pro-Nazi Afrikaaners—the name given to the Dutch settlers. It is his first exposure to racism, which leaves PK upset. Freeman plays a Zulu named Geel Piet who teaches PK how to box and defend himself.

Piet associates PK with the "Rain Man" legend, about a savior who unites the black and white tribes of South Africa. By the time PK is eighteen, he has become an antiapartheid freedom fighter.

Most critics felt the movie, which was partly filmed on location in Zimbabwe and Botswana, was too heavy handed. A 1992 *Seattle Times* review noted, "If the movie didn't make PK into a god, it would help. Given the horror they continue to endure, the blacks of South Africa don't need to be upstaged in their own lives by a white kid, and it does them precious little good to be shown worshipping such a kid. As a young boy hanging around the prison, PK has a unique ability to get people from all the tribes (including white tribes) to get along. But the white imagination that would transform that talent into a god figure for blacks needs to rethink his cosmology. It reduces blacks' experience to entertainment and education for whites."

Freeman admits *The Power of One* did not fulfill its original promise. "That movie was one of those things where . . . well, the script read so well and it looked so wonderful. I had a beautiful expectation for it, but it didn't evolve to be what it was supposed to be. It wasn't as good as I had hoped it would be. I can't say particularly why, but I wasn't as moved as when I was reading the script."

His next project not only lived up to its potential, but also for many far exceeded that potential. Originally titled *The William Munny Killings, Unforgiven* is a postmodern, revisionist Western that shows the true cost of violence—what begins as a thirst for revenge becomes a search for redemption.

Clint Eastwood produced, directed, and starred in the movie, which he told the *New York Times* had been sitting on his shelf a long time.

"I bought the film seven or eight years ago. I kind of nurtured it as a little jewel. I figured I'd age into it a little bit, just have something to look forward to doing. The fellow I play is really living on the edge of hell most of the time. He's really a tormented person."

The movie opens with a prostitute in the dusty town of Big Whiskey circa 1880 getting her face slashed by two drunken cowboys. When the local, morally reprehensible sheriff Little Bill Daggett, played by Gene

Hackman, lets the men off with a slap on the wrist, the outraged town whores pool their money to buy their retribution—one thousand dollars to whoever murders the cowboys.

A young hotshot who calls himself The Schofield Kid enlists former top gunslinger Bill Munny to help him collect the bounty. But Munny's glory days are all but a dim memory. He hung up his guns over a decade earlier and became a peaceful hog farmer after getting married and starting a family. Now a widower with two children, he is struggling both emotionally and financially. Although a deeply changed person who is disengaged from his violent past, the prospect of earning the bounty money to keep his farm and feed his children proves too tempting. Munny enlists the help of his former partner, played by Morgan Freeman, for one last ride. But the men will end up paying a high price for the bounty when they cross paths with Daggett.

Eastwood wasn't interested in depicting violence for its own sake. "Other than just riding and shooting somebody down, there's got to be some meaning behind it all," he told the *New York Times*. "This is the first Western I've ever read where the consequences of violence have been studied, and the pain of it, and the effects on everybody involved, even the perpetrator as well as the victim. If I was ever going to do a last Western, this would be it because it kind of sums up what I feel. Maybe that's why I didn't do it right away. I was kind of savoring it as the last of that genre, maybe the last film of that type for me."

The movie filmed on location in Alberta, Canada and for Freeman, it was "a childhood dream come true—a kid who grew up riding a broomstick riding real horses with Clint Eastwood and Gene Hackman!"

Until I was fifteen years old, the first thing I would put on in the morning after I put my pants on was my gun belt. I spent entire summers riding a broom handle. I kid you not. I did not get on a real horse until I was nineteen. I'd ride tree limbs, fences. . . .

One of my favorite movies was the first western Clint directed, *The Outlaw Josey Wales*. I loved Clint's work, because there's always that hint of darkness in the middle of something

seemingly normal. . . . Seeing him in those Sergio Leone westerns, I felt like, *Man, I'd love to do one of those.*

Freeman reveals that he might have missed his chance to work on
Unforgiven if it hadn't been for Eastwood's determination.

"I was in Africa, negotiating to do another picture that ended up
not having enough money. The producer for *Unforgiven* called me
telling me that my agent was trying to price me out of a career so I
said all right, that I'd have a word with my agent. Put in the call, back
and forth, didn't get a call back somewhere along the line and
thought *All right, that's that.* Then Clint calls me and made an offer,
same offer they were making before but the first time I hear about the
project, which turns out to be, you know, the film that I'd give my left
testicle to do."

Interestingly, the character in the script was not written as a black
man—this was just a case of Eastwood's color-blind casting. Nor does
the script even make mention of his character's race. "That would have
been apologetic," says Freeman, "so I'm grateful for that."

When told by one reporter he had brought dignity to the role, Freeman expressed a blip of frustration. "It has nothing to do with me. I
don't know anything about that. It's not like I wake up in the morning and say, *I got to be dignified today.* If the characters seem dignified,
it's because they were written that way. I don't want to go around talking about how I feel about honesty and all that stuff, but if you can
find where the kernel of a character's soul is, if you can somehow
plumb that, then it's easy to play. I think that sense of dignity has to
do with the fact that there's an inner life that's readable more than
anything else."

Freeman remembers the first time he ever met Eastwood, the day he
showed up on the *Unforgiven* set. "I'd never seen him in person, met him
on the set, and practically genuflected. He said '*Welcome*' and the next
thing was, '*We'll be working together tomorrow.*' That was it."

But their rapport was immediate. "What I like most about Clint is
the great feeling on the set," says Freeman. "Because he trusts the

material, and he trusts you. . . . He hires you because he believes you can do it. He spends his time on other things, like getting the film made. He doesn't direct the actors. He directs the film."

Eastwood admits that in many ways *Unforgiven* is a morality play couched as a western.

"Most of the Westerns I've read don't discuss that at all," he explained to the *Boston Globe*, referring to the moral ambiguity of Munny's character. "Usually, you're dealing with the protagonist who goes around and can't wait to right the wrongs, but he doesn't have any qualms about it one way or the other. There's no conscience of it at all. It starts out with the women's-rights issue and the lack of justice for women as second-class citizens, and that sets into motion a snowball of events that are just fatalistic. There's no way you can stop that wheel from turning. . . . It's how all these circumstances kind of compile and end up with nine people getting killed, not all of them bad people, undeserving of death. But like William Munny says, '*Deserving's got nothing to do with it.*' It's actually antiviolence."

In a word, Eastwood is diametrically opposite from John Wayne— figuratively and literally. "We made different kinds of films," he observed to writer Jay Carr. "He was always very heroic. . . . I've done more mythic kinds of stuff. I know he didn't like *High Plains Drifter*. . . . He wrote me a letter telling me he didn't like it. He said that picture had nothing to do with the people who settled the West, and all that sort of thing. My answer to it would have been, *Of course, it doesn't because it wasn't intended to. It was a fable.* But he's a man of another generation. He came up with a different ideal. This is why I never sat down and argued about it—or replied."

Even the appeal of the western has taken on a new patina. "Now everything's so complicated, so mired down in bureaucracy that people can't fathom a way of sorting it out," Eastwood mused in a *Seattle Times* interview. "In the West, even though you could get killed, it seems more manageable, like a lone individual might be able to work things out some way. In our society today, the idea of one person making a difference one way or the other is remote."

Although an uncomfortable film to watch, audiences and critics were riveted. Desson Howe's review in the *Washington Post* summed up the film's impact.

> *Unforgiven* dismounts at places usually left in the dust—the oppressed lot of women, the loneliness of untended children, adult illiteracy and the horrible last moments of the dying. Never did deaths count so much in a gun-slinging drama; never did shooting a man come so hard. . . .
>
> *Unforgiven* jumps adroitly between the macho and anti-macho, the romantic and anti-romantic. . . . The finale, in which all moral safeties are taken off and the barrels get to blaze, is more of a blood-justice conclusion than a heroic shootout. Travis Bickle of *Taxi Driver* seems to be hovering somewhere in the ether. That things don't end gloriously, that morals lie dangling, is all to the movie's credit. There's a price to killing, we're being shown, that never quite gets paid.

The film won the Academy Award for best picture and earned Eastwood his first best director award. Hackman was also honored with a best supporting actor Oscar. Freeman admits he was a bit surprised at the film's success. "I thought we had all the fun we were going to have in making it."

Backstage it became clear why Eastwood and Freeman had bonded so quickly—they shared a fundamental philosophy about life and work. "You have to take the work seriously, not yourself too seriously—and that only comes with time."

8

IT'S AN OLD cliché that every actor wants to direct. It might be more accurate to say that over the course of a career, many actors come across one project they are so passionate about they want to bring it to screen with their unique vision.

For Freeman, neither scenario fit. He says it was mostly serendipity that he ended up directing *Bopha!*, based on the semiautobiographical play by Percy Mtwa about a black South African policeman—like Mtwa's own father—who comes to a crisis of conscience over his role in enforcing apartheid. The play, first performed in South African townships, was eventually staged at the National Theater in London. When producer Larry Taubman attended an American production at the Los Angeles Arts Festival in 1986, he became committed to bringing the story to film. It would take the better part of a decade.

"I went around to the American film market," Taubman told writer Judy Gerstel, "and I pitched this maybe 100 times. And I realized all they were really interested in were the action/adventure elements in it." Part of the resistance was the poor track record of apartheid films such as *Cry Freedom*. But Taubman blamed the bad box office on "the reluctance to tell the story from the point of view it needed to be told," namely, from the black perspective.

It was only after Arsenio Hall came aboard as executive producer that Paramount—the studio producing his then-late night talk show—backed the project. Originally, Freeman was approached to play the lead, but his agent suggested this might be the perfect opportunity to let his client try his hand at directing. Once Freeman learned Danny Glover—best known for the *Lethal Weapon* film series—and Alfre Woodard had been signed, he committed, consummating a long flirtation.

"I'd been looking at the idea kind of sideways," Freeman says. "This one fell into my lap when I thought I was mentally prepared to try it. When you're an actor, you get into a movie, hit hard and move on. Directing just goes on and on after everyone else has left. But I liked the idea of going back to Southern Africa, and that was far enough away from the overseers (in Hollywood)."

Directing appealed to him on a more personal level as well. "I grew up going to movies. And found no representation of myself. I didn't wonder why not. It was a fact of life. Things come in their own time, and when they do, you seize it."

The producers offered Freeman the starring role as well, but he felt that "Danny's connection to Africa is much deeper than mine. His power and ability work much better for this character than mine would."

Beyond that, Freeman admits the idea of acting in a film he was directed had no appeal. "I'd seen that done. I'd just seen Clint do it in *Unforgiven*. I worked with Kevin Costner right after he had done it. The project comes out fine—and you're just about dead."

Set in 1980, a police officer named Micah Mangena is forced to confront his priorities and beliefs after his teenage son Zweli joins a militant antiapartheid group. Their opposing views threaten to rip the family apart.

"Micah believes he is doing the right thing in upholding the law," observes Freeman. "He has ideals of furthering and bettering the lives of the people in his community, even though those ideals have little to do with the reality of his job. When he finds himself having children arrested and shot and sees fellow police officers slinging *sjamboks* (a kind of club) across the backs of women, he realizes he cannot ignore the realities of the situation any longer. It's a two-edged sword, being a policeman, being black and part of the system that is set up to keep South African Blacks under the hammer of apartheid. On one hand, here's a man who has a good job; on the other hand, he's like a watch dog that the employer oppresses."

Bopha!—the Zulu word for *arrest* which is also a colloquial protest expression—was the first major apartheid film presented from a black viewpoint. But the overt political aspects of the issue were less the focal point of the film than the human element—a clear effort to keep the movie from being seen as merely a *black film.*

The world is made up of an awful lot of people. They're all one thing. They're all one organism. We're all hairs on one dog.

The story could have been set anywhere, but this was written by a black South African from the inside—not from the standpoint of looking in from the outside. We're inside the family's home, we eat with them, spend time in school, in the police station with Micah the father, and at work with Rosie the mother. We get to know this family and watch them pay the price for Micah's involvement.

Although to some Glover's cop may not be a particularly sympathetic character, Freeman sees him as an "everyman" caught up in a situation out of his control.

"A man does the best he can for himself and his family, and [being a policeman] was better than working in the mines down there, and it's better than a lot of things you could choose to do. It's an honorable profession. He thought of himself as being in a position of some help rather than being an oppressor. So, that's giving him every benefit of the doubt. That you get caught in the middle of a situation that you can't control—sometimes your choices rear up and bite you in the butt, so to speak."

In keeping true to the original material, Freeman had to understand the dynamics of a South African family.

> We had to be careful that this family didn't have American values, American family dynamics. In this country, the mother and father are at the top—we see the hierarchy in our families being father and mother pretty much on a level line and then down to the children. But there it's father, son, mother, daughter. It's mostly a matter of attitude, the way they relate to each other. And so that becomes a reality that you have to function with emotionally.
>
> This is not like anything I've experienced. No one who has lived in the United States can know what it is like to live in South Africa.

And it was his effort to be true to the time and place depicted in the film that prompted Freeman to insist on script changes prior to shooting because after his first scouting trip to Africa he realized the script was too sanitized. When he, Glover, and Woodard traveled to Johannesburg, Freeman says they met with "policemen's wives, all ex-wives, and learned how horribly these women lived. We learned a lot about the truths of the situation . . . and here we have this hero that we've already taken a lot of liberties with. I mean, there was never a time during apartheid where a black sergeant had any kind of power and they would never have taken someone that they'd arrested and given him a badge. So once that research was done and we got back together, we all decided that we needed rewrites—we had *Ozzie and Harriet* in Africa, an American-style nuclear family with the Western patriarchal hierarchy. Then we had this sort of easygoing family drama with no tension at anytime in the picture. So we got the rewrites going, they were going along just fine, and finally get to the ending and it just wasn't going to work."

The way it was written, Glover's character would survive—something Freeman says simply wasn't honest. "The film starts with a neck-lacing, man—the guy's got to die. There's no other ending for him. . . . So I get this call from the producers who say that under no circumstances does Danny die. But I did it the way that I saw it and that's what we did—no matter what, you have to empower yourself and for good or for bad, that's my movie and nobody else's. It's not to say that I didn't need encouragement and support, I did—and courage. But if it's yours be sure that it's yours."

The movie filmed in Zimbabwe, despite having been cleared to shoot in South Africa, which at the time was slowly phasing out apartheid. But with emotions running high in the country, the film-makers thought it prudent to steer clear—especially because the insurance premium would have been prohibitively expensive.

While Freeman was pleased to be back in Zimbabwe, where he had filmed *The Power of One*, he was struck again by the terrible poverty afflicting the country. "It's tough to see people who cannot feed their own families and the thing that's hard for people from pampered societies to come to grips with is how much others struggle to survive in certain parts of the world."

The jobs they were able to offer the locals were deeply appreciated he says. "Coming there to make a movie and offering all this work we were very welcome there, and if you hire people, boy they just did it all day."

Alfre Woodard, who played Glover's wife Rosie, says filming in Africa was a revelation. "As soon as I got inside, much of my work was done for me. No longer did I have to imagine the inconvenience, the anguish, the humiliation, the disparity between people's lives. In that sense it fed what I was doing as an actor, but also once you get inside there's so much life, people are so welcoming, in a sense you understand how colonization was possible all those centuries in Africa because people have a different relationship to ownership, to land, to possessions. People are very open, very warm and sharing, and they don't demand any credentials. No amount of degradation, brutality and neglect have snuffed out the spirit of the African people."

Prior to the start of filming, the actors spent two week rehearsing, which Freeman says "is a luxury for a movie. . . . We were able to sit around the table and read through the scenes and discuss them. Then, when the actors get to the set, they remember the discussion—not the exact words, but the intent."

In trying to find his directing style, Freeman became what he called a "third eye. When you're on stage, the audience fills that function for you. On film your whole audience is the director and cinematographer. Actors don't know all the time what they're showing, so I tell them what I see and make general suggestions. Often I'll just ask, '*What are you feeling? What are you thinking?*' so I'll know better what they're trying to get across. Then I say to them, '*This is what I see*'—that's helping to shade and guide a performance."

He also relied heavily on his experiences as an actor. "I think having control is having kid gloves and a very light grip. The biggest task for a director is to stay out of the way as much as possible. I knew that because I was an actor. And because I'd worked with some directors who are masters of staying out of the way: Bruce Beresford, Walter Hill, Clint Eastwood. As you go through working with people, there are those who influence you one way or another, and I think subconsciously they become embedded and resurface later on when you're working."

Freeman says he soon realized the anticipation of directing was more difficult than the actual process. "It's like if you're gonna sail the ocean the first time, you know, the contemplation of it is what is the most daunting. The actual doing is just an everyday doing. You spend a lot of time saying, *That looks fine*, as a director. Your departments come together and they do things and it's magic. Folks walk through this sort of dream starting to coalesce into one thing, all these different people, and the movie grows. It's amazing."

Once he got into the middle of it, Freeman admits to having an epiphany. "And that revelation was that you don't really have that much to do as a director. I have all due respect for them. But that's what the best of them have said—the best being the ones that I like—it's not a big deal to direct. You just have to be there. Someone has to keep it aimed toward that point on the shore."

Freeman readily admits he patterned his style after Clint Eastwood, who he says "is the epitome of how I'd like to direct. He's very collaborative, he has *big ears*, he's laid-back, he uses a professional crew, and he seems not to get in the way. But it's difficult to act and direct as he does. While we were making *Unforgiven*, I watched how the load was shared. He is the best at working with the crew. He works fast without really working hard, and I kind of like that style."

They shot for nine weeks, six days a week, and came in on time and on budget. As its release date neared, the film was the center of a lot of attention from antiapartheid advocates in the United States and abroad. The movie's premiere benefited the African National Congress, although Freeman's view never wavered that *Bopha!* was first and foremost entertainment. Any political consciousness raised was simply a plus—but not something a filmmaker should count on.

I think sometimes you throw the dice and they hit a pebble. Instead of coming up seven, they come three. We hope seven or eleven, of course, but there's no way of saying. And the fact that it's so much in the news may not work for it. You never know. There's no way to second-guess it.

The entertainment industry does not operate on the necessity of social relevance. It operates on what the buying public buys. They'll sell anything if it sells. People are buying entertainment. They're not buying education. That's free. The government provides that. They're not buying social relevance. That's your job. You want it, you go to the church or wherever you go. We can't lay too much social responsibility on the entertainment industry.

Freeman's immediate concerns for the movie's reception were more personal. "I want them to say, 'Ah, I have never seen a movie so well-made.' I want them to say Alfre [Woodard] . . . should be getting an Academy Award; Danny Glover should be getting an Academy Award. This movie should be nominated as one of the 10 best. I want them to say all of the great things about it, of course."

Unfortunately, the movie's reception was decidedly lukewarm. Movie critic Desson Howe wrote, "For viewers unfamiliar with the horrors of apartheid (a distinct minority, one hopes), *Bopha!* should have a powerful effect. But for the most part, there's nothing new here. Every dramatic or political 'discovery' has been unearthed a billion times before, by a steady plurality of South African plays . . . and American movies."

The *Seattle Times* found the movie dull. "Good intentions are famous for paving the road to hell, but more often they just lead to well-meaning tedium. . . . The movie means to address the impossible position of being both black and a policeman in South Africa. Alas, it doesn't so much dramatize this moral dilemma as drain it of its tragic power through repetition. *Bopha!* begins to connect with the true horror of the story only toward the end, and by then it's too late. The movie simply lacks the sense of outrage that propels such powerful antiapartheid movies as *A Dry White Season* and *A World Apart*."

Some of the criticism seemed to generate from Freeman's decision to keep the focus and emotional foundation strictly familial—as if his lack of political fire somehow diffused the action on-screen.

While promoting the film, it was politely suggested that Freeman was intentionally avoiding becoming embroiled in a direct discussion of apartheid or the impending transition of power slowly moving forward in South Africa. "I very well might be," he admitted. "That may be a mind-set that I have. See I don't particularly care for politics, things political. It's a necessity of existence but it fast becomes an *ism*, and I don't deal well with *isms*."

Even if the film is set within a political situation, Freeman stressed that to him,

> The story I think is primarily the tug-of-war between . . . the father and the son—it's generational.
>
> I think the story is about accepting some responsibility for yourself, black or white, and your condition. Up until the time his boy is arrested, Mangena can see no gain for himself in questioning

the choice he has made. It's a job, and he's got one in a place where there are very few. It's very difficult for him to understand why his son would reject the good life. For me, the whole point of the film is what his choices really are.

He tries to defend who he is and what he's doing when he says, *"Can't you understand it's not 'my' law?"* That's a copout because it *is* his law—once you obey it, you embrace it. It's the Nuremberg defense: *I was just obeying orders.* And it won't wash, because you're responsible for what you do.

Bopha! opened in twenty-six theaters on September 24, 1993, and after a month, despite favorable reviews, had only earned a skimpy $200,000 at the box office. Danny Glover, best known for his hugely successful *Lethal Weapon* series opposite Mel Gibson, was dejected, telling *Entertainment Weekly* that Paramount had "given up on it for all intents and purposes."

Freeman was more pragmatic when interviewed by the magazine's Meredith Berkman. "This will go down as Paramount's prestige effort. They weren't looking to make a killing. You can't fault studios for their hesitancy to invest in more esoteric films. You have to make meaningful things that are commercial. Otherwise you're just jerking off, if you'll pardon the expression."

Not all the reviews were negative. Many critics commended Freeman's efforts behind the camera. "Not all actors-turned-directors make the grade, but with *Bopha!* Morgan Freeman proves he is almost as accomplished behind the camera as he is in front of it," wrote Hal Hinson of *The Washington Post.* "Freeman lays out the father-son dynamics with great skill and very little fuss. There's no hysteria in his approach; instead, he sticks to the facts, relying on his cast to provide the emotion. The result is a surprisingly powerful, insightful film. The dramatic curve of the narrative may not seem entirely fresh, and some of the characters are simplistic, but the movie still gets to you."

Although Freeman claimed to have enjoyed the process—"It's fun to be the bride after being the bridesmaid and just a working stiff for so many years. It has its own excitement"—he's not exactly burning to become a actor-director hyphenate.

"It was a great experience on one hand and terrible on another . . . there is a lot of politicking that goes into making a film," such as when it was strongly suggested he make the film more violent—which he resisted.

"I'm spoiled by working in a movie for two or three months and getting paid very well," he said. "By comparison, directors get paid poorly, work up to eighteen months on a film, with someone always breathing down their necks. After all that, a movie critic may wake up in a bad mood and say it's trash. I'll stick to acting."

And back to enjoying his laid-back life in Mississippi. By the early 1990s, Freeman employed five workers to care for his farm and the rest of his land, which now included a small cemetery where his stepfather was buried. One of his favorite pastimes is saddling up one of his horses and going off for daylong rides.

"He'll disappear in the morning with some beef jerky, and I won't see him again until dark," says his wife Myrna.

Inevitably, when Freeman talks about Mississippi, he's asked about lingering racism and Old South attitudes; and just as inevitably he dismisses such concerns and explains that he needed to move back home.

Having traveled around the country, the world, I have discovered that there was no place to go to hide from racism. If it's a problem for you, it's a problem for you. You just find it wherever you are.

I was really sick of the urban scene being packed in with eight million other people, living in a box. . . . I'd go back and sit and realize how absolutely beautiful and peaceful it was. That's how I grew up, just kind of sitting, you know, taking my fishing cane and going down to the creek and catching fish and sitting in the China berry tree and dreaming.

Morgan Freeman and Clint Eastwood during an award ceremony at the American Film Festival of Deauville, France. Eastwood was awarded for his career in film.

Freeman hugs Ashley Judd during a hand and foot print ceremony honoring Freeman at Grauman's Chinese Theater.

Freeman with wife Myrna Colley-Lee at the unveiling of his star on the Hollywood Walk of Fame.

Freeman with daughter Morgana at the 77th Academy Awards ceremony. Freeman was nominated for an Oscar for best actor in Million Dollar Baby.

Producer Arnold Kopleson confers with Brad Pitt and Morgan Freeman on the set of Seven.

Sharts (Jihmi Kennedy), Trip (Denzel Washington), Rawlins (Freeman) and other soldiers square off against jeering white Union troops in Glory.

Keanu Reaves and Morgan Freeman in Chain Reaction.

Fast Black (Morgan Freeman) threatens Jonathan (Christopher Reeve) in Street Smart.

Boolie Werthan (Dan Aykroid) stands with his mother, southern matron Daisy Werthan (Jessica Tandy), and her chauffeur, stalwart and wise Hoke Calhoun (Morgan Freeman) in front of their mansion and 1948 Hudson automobile, in Driving Miss Daisy.

Hibble (Morgan Freeman) takes Flora (Aisling Corcoran) from the orphanage to the New World in Moll Flanders.

Morgan Freeman and Tim Robbins in The Shawshank Redemption.

Bopha!, *in which Freeman both acted and made his directorial debut.*

Lieutenant William Somerset (Morgan Freeman) briefs the police force on the seven deadly sins in Seven.

Morgan Freeman in Million Dollar Baby, *in which he was nominated for best supporting actor.*

You can exist down there without having to hear your neighbor break wind or, for that matter, hear your neighbor. All that moisture can wear some people down, but I live for it.

But being one of Hollywood's most in-demand talents meant that before long, Freeman was packing his bags for his next job, one that would bring him his third Academy Award nomination.

9

IT'S SOMEWHAT KARMICALLY appropriate that one of the country's most prolific writers would be paired up with one of America's busiest actors. Set in 1947, on its face *The Shawshank Redemption* is a prison movie about enigmatic banker Andy Dufresne and his friendship with another con after being convicted to life imprisonment for murdering his cheating wife and her lover. But peeling away the layers, the film becomes a testament to the human spirit, friendship, love, and the power of hope.

Tim Robbins, who stars as Dufresne, told writer Glenn Lovell, "It's about the prison inside us. Everyone has limitations forced on them. We're all told from an early age, *Don't do that. You shouldn't be that. You shouldn't dream that.* It takes a lot of strength, a lot of will, to keep focused . . . to keep the spirit alive."

Based on his 1982 novella, *Rita Hayworth and the Shawshank Redemption*, Stephen King said he was inspired by recollections of prison movies he watched growing up. To prepare for his role, Robbins spent time in a real prison.

"I put on shackles and full prison gear and put my hair in front of my face, and went into solitary," he recalled to Lovell. "I wanted to go for a couple of days, but they would only let me stay in for three hours. I watched the prisoners, talked to the guards. I'll never forget the eyes of one guy I saw in solitary. He must have been eighteen. His eyes were dead; there was no life left in them. None of the prisoners recognized me. The scary thing is that all the prisoners kept yelling out, '*What did you do?*' I didn't lie and say I knocked off a bank. I just didn't talk at all. This made the guys sort of mad. Luckily there wasn't a riot."

The film was written by Frank Darabont, who at thirty-five was making his directorial debut on *Shawshank*, which had a modest $25 million budget. Freeman was the director's first choice for Red, the film's narrator, even though in the short story he was a lily-white Irishman. Red, serving his own sentence for murder, is the prison's resident wheeler-dealer who can supply whatever you want from the outside—for a price.

Freeman says he's never been sure exactly why he was offered the role.

I never ask that, though, because I don't care. What's important is that they did offer it, and I think people still like it because somehow, the whole trilogy of hope, redemption and success comes together for audiences.

It's a love affair. They're not *in love* with each other—they're friends who are interdependent. It's what *Butch Cassidy and the Sundance Kid* and *Thelma & Louise* were about.

I think that's what resonates with people. Some people say it's about hope. But it's a powerful story about a relationship.

He was especially drawn to Red because of the character's shades of gray. "You never actually knew, you accepted him as being a good guy even though he was a confessed murderer. He killed somebody, and the anger when you let go and go that far is immense. You didn't see it and you never did see that part of him, but it was always there."

The production filmed on location during the summer of 1993 in Mansfield, Ohio, with the Ohio State Reformatory doubling for King's fictitious Shawshank State Prison of Maine. The Reformatory had been built in the late nineteenth century and designed to resemble an old gothic German castle; most of the incarcerated prisoners were first-time offenders.

For years, the Reformatory was considered a model prison, but by the 1930s, overcrowding and failing infrastructure began to take its toll. In December 1990, the state of Ohio officially retired it as a prison, and the outbuildings were razed in order to expand the neighboring Mansfield Correctional Institute. In 1995, a local preservation society secured the deed and now hosts tours and overnight "ghost hunts."

Joining the cast were background extras who were no strangers to life behind bars. Ex-cons who had served time at the Reformatory were recruited as were guards to provide added authenticity. Some of the stories told by old-timers painted a bleak picture.

Richard Hall, an assistant warden, told *Entertainment Weekly* that back in the day, the six-foot by eight-foot solitary cells "had nothing but a hole in the floor—no lights. Guys would be in the dark for four days with nothing but bread and water twice a day."

The dilapidated conditions inside the Reformatory heightened the mood of the shoot for the actors—and also seemed to heighten nerves. But Robbins told *Entertainment Weekly* that they found ways to try and release tension, such as the time he was supposed to kill a maggot he found in his oatmeal. "The first time we shot it someone from the ASPCA was on the set because we were using a bird that day. We were informed by the person that we weren't allowed to kill the maggot on screen. So . . . someone made a little matchstick director's chair with a star on it and *Maggot* on the back. We put the maggot on his chair between takes."

Such light moments aside, neophyte director Darabont found himself at odds with his crew—the director of photography felt that panoramic shots of the local landscape detracted from the need to show the inmates' sense of claustrophobia—and cast, notably, Freeman.

Darabont's other struggle was with one of his stars. "For me," Freeman remarks, "someone who comes to the project as a writer first is not going to be a good director. He's going to usurp my job. You pay an actor for his expertise. If you don't use it you'll raise hackles."

Freeman was signed to the movie first and was consulted on possible costars.

They ran a whole bunch of possibilities past me: 'Who do you wanna work with?' Tim Robbins. So it was me and Tim. He is another one of those actors, who, I think he is just transcendent in his work. When he got his teeth into something he is totally watchable. He is absolutely engrossing to me.

Actors who have characters who they totally understand help each other understand even more and I think that was what was happening with us. The deeper we got, the more we shot, the more we understood each other. The bonding was just the normal character thing. Of course we're close friends now.

Tim and I, we work in the same way. When we're in rehearsal or they say roll cameras, we're there, doing our jobs. Otherwise, we're doing other things. He's not a brooder, I'm not a brooder.

Darabont acknowledged to *Entertainment Weekly* that "the director has to gauge what any actor needs." While Robbins enjoyed talking things out, for Freeman, "it boils down to *Where do I sit? Where do I turn?*"

Although Freeman made nice in the pre-release interviews, telling Brownwen Hruska, "Frank Darabont is a writer, but he's not crazy. He's made a wonderful movie," he later expressed his frustration. "That was a strange production. There were moments of extreme tension on the set—between the producers and actors, between the director and actors, between everybody; just this personality stuff between different groups. Very strange."

Specifically, Freeman's issues concerned working with a hyphenate. "I have a problem with writer-directors; personal. I can't work well with both of them on the set, if both of them are giving instructions. Writers tend to be in love with what they wrote. You can't always translate the words into the meaning, sometimes the meaning is better served without the words, difficult to make a writer to try to understand that. It gets, sometimes, tense."

Freeman is also quick to give credit to Darabont for the final product. "I think highly of him. . . . He wrote it, he directed it, it's his movie, his mark and it's a great film."

He also credits Stephen King with creating layered characters that adapted well to film from the printed page. "I think the appeal is there because Stephen is not just a prolific writer but a really good writer, an excellent writer. If you look at the things that were made into movies, they were made into movies because they were really well-drawn character studies. In the scary ones, the ones outside of things like *Shawshank*, what do you want for visuals? Carrie for instance—that was a character."

Freeman acknowledges that often cinematic success has to be measured over time and lasting legacy because opening week movie receipts don't always tell the whole story.

"Everywhere I go, everywhere I go, everywhere I go. People say, *Shawshank Redemption*—best movie I ever saw. It opened the same year that *Dumb and Dumber* opened. It made $35 million at the box office, domestic. *Dumb and Dumber* made $110 million. *Duu-uh*. It's a transcendent moment for us as actors that the movie comes out and becomes what it has become. One of the most watched, one of the most rented videos, I guess in the world."

Even if it took audiences time to find *Shawshank*, critics were immediately enamored. *Washington Post* writer Donna Britt said that Morgan Freeman shared a spiritual connection with legend Sydney Poitier, who "slipped into white America's collective imagination, opening it to the notion of black nobility as he grew stronger and smarter with each role. . . . " Britt continued,

Like Poitier, Freeman has irritated some by playing men whose response to racism is more reasoned than raw—the chauffeur in *Driving Miss Daisy*; the wise Muslim sidekick in *Robin Hood*. In *Shawshank*, the year's most satisfying film, Freeman transforms another seemingly stereotypical role: a black admitted murderer doing hard time. . . .

Thanks in part to Poitier, today's black characters needn't be noble beyond belief to make folks relate to them. But I'm ready for Hollywood to show some redemption of its own: by casting more guys like Freeman as the brainy bankers and Robbins as the convicted killers.

Jay Carr of the *Boston Globe* observed,

As he moves from numbness to a sort of mastery of his environment, Robbins' way of staying interiorized, saying a lot more with his eyes than with his mouth, reminds us of why he's at the forefront of young American actors. . . .

And Freeman, who is second to none at projecting weight and presence, is unforgettable when he stands yet again in front of a parole board he knows will turn him down, indifferent because he knows how many of his own best years he has murdered along with his victim. That two such guarded men would become friends is hardly a foregone conclusion. Yet they do, and believably—because the film has the good sense to create the impression that it happens very slowly, over a period of time. . . .

Robbins and Freeman make what could have been an endurance test an utterly engrossing experience.

Many in Hollywood agreed, and the movie earned Freeman his third Oscar nomination, his second for best actor. Once again, he became the center of media attention and was prodded by a probing press to examine his career. During a press junket, he took the opportunity to give potential employers a goose by telling reporters he felt stereotyped, "partly because folks like you have been pointing it out. I would love to do comedy. A well-rounded thespian—I flatter myself that I fit the description—does comedy. I did a lot on the stage, and I'm good at it. It's also harder to do than people realize, since the immediate payoff is a happy one." But studios never thought to cast him in such roles.

Unfortunately, Freeman says despite his myriad of roles he has been subtly boxed in as a performer. He believes much of that is due to the studio practice of audience testing.

I think I've been pigeonholed. I have *gravitas*. I can't play bad guys. That's unacceptable. It's great to hear that your career has shown a lot of diversity, but it's not really true. People talk about it and say *gravitas* in the next breath. I've gotten a little tired of *gravitas*.

If you're successful playing any kind of character you tend to get offers to play roles like it. I got offered a lot of *Street Smart* roles until *Daisy*. Then I got offered a lot of old man roles.

I'm concerned about being bracketed. But I also realize that all of these roles are ones that I chose to do, so I have to take the responsibility for these choices. Yeah, I like roles that make statements about American life and history, and I always wanted to have that kind of impact. I'm drawn to these kinds of things, and I admit it. But still, I don't want to be shut out of other kinds of roles that don't have quite the . . . gravitas.

I don't get any chance to do humor. I can be sarcastic. It isn't really humor, what you would call comedy. I would like to do different stuff, to have a range. I haven't had one. I might have to drop out for a while and go away.

Freeman says if he's done himself "any favors at all, it has been rejecting those follow-up roles. People say, '*This role was written with you in mind.*' What it really means is that it was written for some character they saw me play."

One reason Freeman loves playing the bad guy is simple. "I'm good at nasty."

In addition to Freeman's nomination, *The Shawshank Redemption* was nominated for best picture. But that year the film was up against the juggernaut known as *Forrest Gump*, which earned a pack-leading thirteen nominations. In the end, *Gump* was too strong, winning six Oscars, including best picture, director, screenplay, and a second consecutive best actor award for Tom Hanks, who had won the previous year as the AIDS-stricken lawyer in *Philadelphia*.

So for the third time, months away from his fifty-eighth birthday, Freeman once again found himself a bridesmaid; he says his attitude about the Oscars became philosophical. "It occurred to me that winning the nomination is probably the height of it. It is pretty much as far as you can go, and the rest of it is pretty much arbitrary."

But time would prove him wrong because as it played out, there was little arbitrary about Freeman's career.

I**T WAS A** testament of his own star power that Morgan Freeman found himself paired with Hollywood golden boy Brad Pitt in 1995's creepfest, *Se7en*. In the disturbing murder thriller, Freeman starred at Lieutenant William Somerset, a weary homicide detective who is biding time until his retirement. For his final week on the force, Somerset is partnered with his replacement, a brash and full of himself young hotshot, David Mills, played by Pitt. But what Mills lacks in experience and wisdom is balanced by a newcomer's enthusiasm for the job that Somerset no longer possesses.

The burnt-out Somerset finds himself in the middle of a gruesome murder investigation. The first victim is an obese man who was literally forced to eat himself to death. A pedophile is chained to his bed and slowly starved. A corrupt lawyer bleeds to death after having a pound of flesh removed from his body.

It doesn't take Sherlock Holmes to figure out these bizarre murders are the work of a serial killer. But it does take Somerset's experience to figure out that each victim represents one of the seven deadly sins—gluttony, sloth, and greed, respectively. The detectives are racing the clock to prevent four more murders representing pride, lust, envy, and wrath. Already convinced our society is morally bankrupt, Somerset says with resigned pessimism, "This isn't going to have a happy ending. It's not possible."

Freeman says he enjoyed the tense older-younger cop dynamic—a fresh departure from the typical buddy-cop film. "I'm the older guy, the thinker. His excitement with this case is the fact that he gets to match wits with someone who thinks he's smart. The killer, John Doe, really thinks he's brilliant. . . . William Somerset offered a challenging depth and dimension for a character in this genre. . . . He is very much like an actor who wants to have a smattering of all knowledge in order to do his job properly."

Even though the story was unrelentingly bleak, Freeman says the role was "very, very immediate to me. It's a story that borders on fantasy because we were in a non-identifiable place in almost a phantasmigorical situation. I mean, imagine someone deciding that he's going to murder seven people for seven reasons. It had a great plot."

Freeman admits it wasn't until an interviewer pointed it out that Somerset and John Doe, the killer, shared a similar view of the world. The only difference is the way in which they have tried to correct society's problems.

There was a moment in *Se7en* when they're driving out into the desert, and John Doe is talking about why he did what he did and . . . Somerset is asking these little low-key questions and watching and listening, but I think he is also thinking, *Hmmm, you can't really argue with that . . . I see that.*

There are people out there who we look at them and say, "*Gosh, why are they even living?*" We don't start plotting to get rid of them, but we do that. So that was a parallel in that the world we're in—Somerset's character was brought on by the same things that are driving John Doe to commit his crimes that he's committing.

Although their on-screen relationship was often strained, off-camera Freeman says Pitt was "delightful; one of those people you look forward to coming to the set because he's ready to work," and denies reports that surfaced during filming that the two actors clashed.

"That's rumor. We never actually disagreed. We had moments where we had difficulty getting the shot, getting the scene done, but I don't recall that we ever had any serious tension between us. There might have been one moment when I opened my mouth once too often . . . but Brad and I got along. He's a professional. I was nowhere near that in my twenties or thirties. I got my first job in the theater at thirty. Still, he's level. He's here to do the work."

Also making an appearance on the set was Freeman's son Alphonse, who had a small role as a fingerprint technician in the film.

Despite the apparent camaraderie among the cast, the shoot was often physically taxing because of the film's stylized atmosphere. *People* magazine reported, "The set was dark, uncomfortable and unhealthy. The director, David Fincher, and others developed a chronic cough because of the water and mineral oil that was blown into the air to create the murky atmosphere."

To achieve the dark, bleak look of the film, Freeman says Fincher also processed the film stock differently.

He is very computer literate, graphic oriented, knows all about film . . . so he was going to do a reclamation process, where you would take all of the silver nitrate that comes out of the wash when you develop the film, run it back through again, which takes the shaded, the dark parts of the movie and makes it darker. That just dampens down the entire movie. The light, the colours, makes it deeper. That is what he did. The problem with the process is that in the newer theaters, they have a different lighting system than the old arc light, that were in the reel to reels. So in those you have to pump it way up in order to get the light, because if you don't, people really can't see.

Unlike many actors who carry their characters home, Freeman says he had no problem leaving Somerset and the movie's disturbing plot behind at the end of each day. "I seldom get into the mood of the story. It's acting. I go in, I act, I quit. I don't take anything away from it."

But according to Fincher, he certainly adds to any film he's in. "Everybody knows Morgan is great. He's a director's dream," he told the *New York Times*.

Morgan never feels the need to prove anything. He doesn't even try to be the center of attention. *Well, why don't I just stand over here?* he might say, meaning off to the side. He's confident that he can command attention over there. He embodies wisdom. He's one of those people who knows how to live, not just how to survive. That comes through. . . .

It was funny working with him and Brad, because Brad is young and restless, always trying to reinvent everything. He evolves hourly. He'll give you fifteen different looks in a scene. Morgan will give you seven or eight subtle variations on a precise mood or emotion.

One of the shoot's lighter moments came at Pitt's expense. At the time, he was romantically involved with costar Gwyneth Paltrow, who plays his sweet-souled—and doomed—wife in the movie. While filming, *People* named Pitt the sexiest man alive and Freeman admits, "We rode Brad about it. The cast gave him a director's chair that said *[Sexiest Man in the Universe]*. I ranted, '*What am I, chopped liver? How dare they insult me by putting this here!*' We [finally] let Brad in on the joke."

After which Paltrow then famously cracked to *Entertainment Weekly*, "Everyone is making all this fuss over Brad but I'm telling you, Morgan Freeman is the sexiest man alive. You heard it here."

Se7en was one of those appreciate-it-or-hate-it films—it was too brutal and disturbing for anyone to truly "love" it. And even those critics who appreciated it seemed unsettled that they did.

"While one can't deny that *Se7en* is a visually stylistic film that lingers long in the memory, one may also only be barely able to comprehend why one sat through it," observed reviewer Beverley Bare Buehrer.

But somewhere in the most primal heart of each of us is the person who drives slowly past road accidents—not because we are concerned for the safety of those who stop to help, but to see a fate that might have been ours. Watching *Se7en* is like gawking at an accident. We may not want to see the wreckage, but we can't seem to turn our heads. . . .

However, undoubtedly the most outstanding element of this film is Morgan Freeman's performance—and it can overcome virtually any of the film's problems. He is a marvel to watch in action.

His portrayal of the intelligent yet world-weary Somerset is a subtly shaded and moving performance. While Pitt is filling the screen with obscenities and an almost unfocused energy, Freeman involves the viewer through his underplayed pauses and glances and his softly delivered pearls of wisdom. This may make the two characters balance each other in the film, but it is Freeman's performance we admire and remember.

The Dallas Morning News made it clear that it wasn't only Pitt's character who had a lot to learn from an older mentor.

Mr. Freeman performs with the tired grace of someone who mistakenly thinks he has encountered every form of mayhem. He embellishes his role with delightful small touches, as when he sits at his typewriter, determinedly hunting and pecking at the keyboard.

Mr. Pitt, minus the exquisite lighting that made him seem like an icon-in-the-making in *Legends of the Fall*, offers a solid portrayal. But in a climactic scene when he must confront a truly horrific situation, his reactions are no more than adequate.

Janet Maslin was more blunt in her *New York Times* critique.

Mr. Freeman moves sagely through *Se7en* with the air of one who has seen it all and will surely be seeing something better very soon. His performance has just the kind of polish and self-possession that his costar, Mr. Pitt, seems determined to avoid. Demonstrating an eighth sin by frittering away an enormously promising career, Mr. Pitt walks through this film looking rumpled and nonchalant, mumbling his lines with hip diffidence to spare. He remains too detached to show much enthusiasm, except for times when the screenplay begins moralizing about what a sick world we live in. Films like this one . . . aren't making it any better.

Ironically, Freeman doesn't disagree, saying about *Se7en*, "There's all this loss and angst and death and sense of helplessness in that movie—if I saw it in the theater, I probably wouldn't have liked it. I saw [director David Fincher's] *Fight Club* and I didn't like it much. It's a great movie, well made, fabulous acting, but it just made me feel so bad. But Fincher is an extraordinarily good director."

As to whether *Se7en* is trying to make a statement about contemporary society as some reviewers suggest, Freeman shrugs it off. "I don't want the audience to get a message. I just want them to get their money's worth."

While on the set all the actors may be been equals, at the film's premiere in New York, Freeman says he was given a potent dose of Sexiest Man Alive reality.

"The press were in my face, and you could see the excitement. And someone said, *Brad Pitt!* and whoop! Just like that, I was standing alone. That was very informing."

Not only was Freeman getting shortchanged by the paparazzi and media. According to a May 1995 survey conducted by *Entertainment Weekly*, Freeman was named one of the most underpaid actors in Hollywood.

"Freeman's recent salary and asking price per film is between $5–6 million when he should earn $11.4 million," reported the magazine. "Other Black actors who earn less than they should included noted actors Samuel L. Jackson, who asks for $4.5 million but should earn $8.4 million, and Danny Glover, who asks for $2 million but should earn $4.8 million."

The good news was that more black actors than ever were working in mainstream films, being cast in roles that traditionally had been an all white boy's club. While Morgan Freeman had been enjoying color-blind casting for years, in 1996 it was only starting to filter down to other black actors.

"It's natural evolution," Freeman believes. "Black actors, just now, belong to the mainstream. The next push is probably going to be for Asian performers, or whoever the next group is struggling to break that unstated barrier. Black actors have broken through."

Not everyone was so optimistic. Referring to Will Smith's turn in *Independence Day*, talent manager Dolores Robinson observed to *Entertainment Weekly*, "I know out there in the black world it's a big thing because it's the first time in the history of film that a black man has saved the world. But do I think it does anything for a lot of black actors? No, I think it does something for those individual people who happen to be in movies that score big bucks at the box office."

Producer Helena Echegoyen agreed. "To me it was shocking to listen to people at Fox talk about how shocked they were with the success of *Waiting to Exhale*," she vented to writer Rebecca Ascher-Walsh. "It was a book that had been on the best-seller list for a year. It had a cameo by Wesley Snipes. It starred Angela Bassett, an Oscar-nominated actress, and Whitney Houston, a worldwide music-industry figure who was in a little $300 million picture called *The Bodyguard*. I mean, what were they thinking?"

Jack Valenti, the former president of the Motion Picture Association of America, defended the industry, saying it was far more concerned with box office than skin color.

"This is the least discriminatory business I know," he told *The Washington Post*. "The question they are thinking about is: Can I make a picture and have it open at $12 to $25 million the first weekend?"

Producer Debra Martin Chase echoed his sentiments, with one notable qualifier. "There's more colorblind [sic] casting than ever before, and the number of black actors and actresses that Hollywood considers popular enough to build a movie around is growing. And yet—it is not enough."

Typically, Freeman chose to stay out of the fray and continued to push Hollywood's doors open through his work instead of through his words. He also seemed to compensate his low-ball paydays by simply working twice as much as everybody else. After appearing in the virus save-the-world thriller *Outbreak*, Freeman costarred in the period piece, *Moll Flanders*, playing a manservant named Hibble who works for Moll's madam.

Freeman decided Hibble should have shoulder-length dreadlocks and conferred with his daughter Deena, who works as his personal hair-stylist on films. "I told my daughter . . . about the look I wanted and told her . . . I had seen it on a young man who does a soap opera. She said, 'Oh yes, I know that, I can do that.' So, I don't always admit it, but I steal, I borrow, I use whomever."

The movie starred Robin Wright as Moll Flanders and was directed by Pen Densham, with whom Freeman had worked on *Robin Hood*. Densham later admitted to the *Dallas Morning News* that Freeman came to the rescue on a day when the director was having a mental block on how to film a particular scene.

"I glanced over at Morgan, and he mapped out the camera movement with a swoop of his fingers. I went up and hugged him because he had given me my solution. I'm scratching my head to figure out how to get him in my next picture."

Moll Flanders was a labor of love for Densham, who had long envisioned bringing his adaptation of DeFoe's novel to the big screen. Unfortunately, the film lacked enough dramatic bite and quickly disappeared from theaters, but Freeman had no regrets because the movie had been an opportunity to educate the audience that blacks have been an important part of history—an issue he feels passionate about.

It's incumbent upon us, I think, to go back as often as possible and look into our past. . . . Growing up I, like a lot of other Americans—black and white—learned an awful lot of history from the movies. I learned . . . the Indians were the bad guys, white women were to be protected at all costs and all we did through life was sing and pick cotton.

Then as years went by, I wondered why as a child I didn't have a better image of myself. I'd then find all these tidbits of information in the corner of somebody's library. I'd go, Why didn't learn this as a child? Lewis and Clark did do the whole mapping thing to the U.S., but it would have been impossible without the help of an Indian woman and a Black man. Yeah, Admiral Perry went to the North Pole, but in the arms of Matthew Alexander Henson. . . . The list is endless of the contributions we made.

So when some questioned the inclusion of a black character not found in the book, Freeman countered by asking, "Why not a Black guy? It's most important you do these kinds of things. That's the reason, the ultimate reason for living, to correct those things that have either been eliminated or falsified, and to elevate."

And with each succeeding film role, Freeman found new ways to elevate both his craft and his Hollywood profile.

11

IN SOME WAYS making a movie is a crap shoot because there are so many variables that go into the final product that the actor has no control over. Even if the original script shows promise, the cast is top notch, and the director skilled, a film may not live up to its potential simply because something is off in the chemistry. *Chain Reaction* was such a project.

The plot centered around a discovery to produce energy cheaply, cleanly, and easily from water. Freeman's character, Paul Shannon, owns the company that funded the project run by two young scientists, Eddie and Lily, played by Keanu Reeves and Rachel Weisz. Of course, some shadowy group wants to prevent the new energy breakthrough from ever being implemented.

On the printed page, Freeman says Shannon was an interesting, nuanced character. "He is an extremely wealthy individual with very high echelon contacts, who has a lot of power. Couple all of that with his relationship to Eddie, and I saw a lot of possibilities with this role."

But his enthusiasm dimmed slightly when he showed up on location is Chicago during a record-breaking winter cold snap. "It was difficult for everyone, particularly for me because I'm tropical. I don't do cold weather. This is Chicago . . . in the winter. I was actually ill and in bed four days at a crack. It was really rough."

Director Andrew Davis told *Jet* that Freeman's professionalism never wavered despite the physical challenges of the shoot and working while sick. "I had always admired Morgan Freeman, and I discovered he is probably one of the greatest actors I'll ever have a chance to work with. He's a gifted collaborator, an inspiration to others and a wonderful human being. In spite of some very tough conditions, he made every-thing easy for all of us."

Although Freeman always maintained he was an actor first and fore-most, in January 1996 he heeded the advice of others and formed his own production company, Revelations Entertainment with Lori McCreary, who had served as a coproducer on *Bopha!*

"Everyone I've talked to that's been successful said it was the only way to get your own projects going. Otherwise, you're at the mercy of others."

Based in Santa Monica, California, the company's official mission statement is to produce "commercially successful entertainment in all existing and emerging media that endeavors to entertain, enlighten and glorify the human experience."

"A project has to hit us in the gut or the heart," says McCreary, who serves as the company's CEO. "We don't have a special genre or any budget range. We're into packaging good stories with good writers to make good movies."

Freeman adds, "The idea was to make movies that would inform as well as entertain because so much of our history is taught through the entertainment medium."

His pet project was to make a film based on the young adult novel by Robert Peck, *A Day No Pigs Would Die*, a coming-of-age story set in the depression about an eighteen-year-old boy and the death of his father. "I figured the way to get it done is to direct it. The story inspired me. Like *Bopha!*, some of these movies you do because you want to see the film get made," Freeman says. "You don't build a studio on them. I read the book and loved it. With the right combination of events and people, every once in a while you get something like *Driving Miss Daisy* or *Tender Mercies*."

But Freeman soon learned that securing funding for small, independent films could be a lengthy and frustrating experience. Although Revelations was able to find a backer willing to cover 65 percent of the projected $7 million budget, the production company was ultimately unable to cover the remaining costs, and after years of effort, the project was scrapped.

"I had a studio executive tell me that it's better for them to make two movies at $40 million apiece than four movies at $20 million apiece," Freeman says.

Acting work kept Freeman from dwelling too much on his producing disappointment, and he worked back to back on several films that ranged from the kitsch to the forgettable to the important to the box office hit.

In *Deep Impact*, the world faced imminent destruction by a comet headed for a direct hit, and Freeman is Tom Beck, the president of the United States who must help save the day.

"When I was doing press for *Deep Impact*, reporters would always ask me how it felt to play the first black President, and I'd tell them, '*I'm not playing the first black President. I'm playing a President who happens to be black.*' Or they'd ask me what sort of research I did for the role. Research? What kind of research do you need to play the President? He's a guy. Truman was a haberdasher. Eisenhower was a soldier. Reagan was an actor. Besides, we all know what Presidents are like standing up there in a press conference. Hell, you don't have to do any research to play a President."

Although audiences readily accepted Freeman as leader of the free world, Freeman notes sardonically, "If you're just pretending, they can handle it. As long as they don't have to actually go and vote for me, it's okay!"

But addressing questions regarding race in America more seriously, Freeman says, "I am going to stop here a moment and try to be intelligent. You're never going to get away from being a black actor or a Chinese actor or an Asian actor or whatever your ethnicity might be. But Hollywood, or I should say the industry itself, is keeping up with the fact that we now have jet airplanes and the Internet and all that, so we're tending to see not in these groupings. And so I try to exploit that fact— I don't have to say I'm black, in other words, do I?"

He also reasserts his previously expressed belief that being black has not been a hindrance—because he hasn't allowed it to be.

"I developed a philosophy over the years, different from the one I was learning growing up. That is, most times you're your own worst enemy. If I give you an excuse to fail, you'll always grab on to it. . . . Because you're definitely going to fall. People without a net don't dare let go. Whatever profession you sign on is net-free—the profession is you and it's you who has to deliver. The best security is insecurity, because it keeps you paying attention. Walking on the edge is much better than walking on flat ground; you pay close attention every step of the way."

While there was absolutely no indication his career was at all slowing down, Freeman admits he takes nothing for granted. "When you're hot, you better go to work, because it's not going to be there for you later. The reality of life is that tomorrow the phone does not have to ring. No question about it. And I don't care how well-known you are, I don't care how famous you are, the day is right around the corner when nobody thinks about you. They think about somebody like you, maybe, but not about you. So every job's your last. That's still true."

But career aside, Freeman is aware his blessings are plentiful.

I enjoy sailing. I enjoy riding my horse. Every morning I saddle my horse and get up on him and ride; I'm very aware, beneath my chaps and my spurs and my hat, I'm doing what I always dreamed I would. Without riding the range and wandering around looking for work, I'm a cowboy for a couple of hours.

I'm not one of those who thinks what they're doing is above and beyond what it really is. It's just pretend. It's play-acting. It's not hard work. Acting is always acting. It's always easy. The hard work is staying with it long enough to become successful. I count success as going a full year without having to work in an office, or do a dish, or drive a cab, or wait tables.

Freeman thinks back to 1965, "and I remember watching this other dancer get his W-2 forms together. He had made $10,000 in 1964! *God, if the time ever comes when I make that much, hey, forget about it!* My income was about $2,500. "I can remember times of being on the street in Los Angeles . . . and being just one day away from begging. At those times you never really think you're going to wind up here, doing this, from this vantage point."

Freeman believes success is largely kismet.

What governs us? Luck. Luck is your only savior. Pluck has something to do with it, but luck decides. One section of the ocean is calm, another section is stormy.

When you're young, you dream, and your dreams are based on what you see on *Lifestyles of the Rich and Famous*. You get inputs that build up one side of the picture. You don't get the alcoholism and the drug overdose. You don't see one thing that's happened to me, the fact that your lucky success points up others' unlucky failure.

I was lucky that my time came when I was best prepared for it to come. I didn't have enough sense, not enough control over myself, back when I wanted success so badly. I would have handled it poorly then. I hope I'm doing better now.

Freeman says the most salient thing about his life is that all his dreams have come true. "I have all the toys I ever wanted, which is not that many. I have a nice car, a nice boat, nice horses, nice wife, nice kids, nice grandkids, nice house, nice home. If it can be called being *there*, then I'm *there*. And if it stops tomorrow, it's a nice time to die."

It's easy to see why Freeman jumped at the chance to appear in *Hard Rain*, a hybrid of an action movie and disaster flick—for the first time since *Street Smart* he was cast as a bad guy, a would-be robber named Jim. The plan is for Jim and his gang to steal $3 million from an armored car during a torrential rain that has flooded the town. But they are stymied by a security guard, played by Christian Slater, who proves willing to protect the cash at any cost.

The movie got some unexpected publicity when Slater was arrested in August 1997 for assaulting his girlfriend and a police officer during a wild party at his home, later admitting he was under the influence of drugs. He was sentenced to three months in jail and began serving his time the day after the *Hard Rain* premiere. When asked if Slater's personal problems had spilled over onto the set, Freeman was supportive of his troubled costar.

"I think Christian has a very clear idea of what is going on in his own head. There was nothing in his work on the film which suggested he had problems with drugs. But work is one thing, play is another. I am surprised sometimes, at the depth of angst that exists for some people." He's also aware of a *there but for the grace of God* reality. "I feel very lucky I've got through life without any major gaffes. I often think I am probably quite lucky that I wasn't a wild success early on, coming up through the seventies. I could have very easily burned out."

The *Hard Rain* shoot was damp but otherwise unremarkable. The majority of the movie was filmed in an abandoned aircraft hangar that housed a six hundred-foot long water tank.

"The film was originally called *The Flood*," says Freeman, "but the studio changed that because it sounded too much like a disaster movie, like *Volcano*. And it's much more character driven than that suggests."

Even so, most of the action takes place in water. "We certainly had to get wet," Freeman acknowledges.

The water power was coming down at six thousand gallons a minute. But from the actor's point of view it wasn't a difficult movie to make. Ask me about hardship and I'll say I didn't have any, although the crew did. They were working all day, every day, and were in the water constantly for at least twelve hours— sometimes for as much as thirty hours at a stretch.

But every time we did a shot, we got out of the water, took our wet clothes off, dried off. Then we could put on some new clothes, and go sit in our trailer until the next scene we were needed for.

As might be expected, in the original script the robbers get their comeuppance at the end, including Jim, who dies. But when producers screened the film prior to release, test audiences were outraged that Freeman's character dies, so the ending was reshot so that Jim gets away. Freeman is still fascinated at the reaction.

It's a weird thing, a strange dichotomy. We started back in the seventies having criminals get away with certain crimes—*Topkapi*, *Thomas Crown Affair I*—people we like pulling off heists and getting away. And we screen *Hard Rain* and we got people not just wanting me to get away, but to get paid. And once the audience says they don't like the ending, some producers heel. Not only do I have to live . . . I have to get some cash for my troubles.

It's a scary thing, and people need to start to think about the messages that they send in the movies. The greatest teaching medium of all time and here we're sending these messed-up messages.

Me, I was doing a job. I'm a working actor first thing, but some days the Twilight Zone of the Subjunctive Mood is the only thing keeps me from going crazy.

More than anything, it reaffirmed to Freeman why producers shied away from casting him as villains.

I have to reconcile myself to the saintliness and those are the offers I get. I'd much prefer more eclectic roles. As an actor you always want to stretch yourself, to go beyond points you have been before. But I have gotten this mantle where people talk about me in the same breath as Spencer Tracy and you don't want to stand up and rail against that.

Growing up, you want to be an actor, and then having grown up and become an actor, for someone to mention my name and Spencer Tracy's in the same sentence is, like, life-affirming. But I don't walk around thinking of myself like *The Old Man and the Sea*, or anything like that.

It's all about working. I may be better trained in being able to do classical work, or being able to speak well enough to do Shakespeare or Brecht or what have you, but it's all one thing—it's acting; it's entertainment.

What am I? I'm a journeyman actor.

Which is precisely why Freeman is always extremely appreciative whenever his work is recognized, such as when the Deauville Film Festival honored him with the Actors Tribute in 1997.

"They contacted me about the honor they were going to give Arnold Kopelson, who's a good friend of mine," Freeman says. "They wanted to know if I would come over and be there when Arnold got his honor. Then they wanted to know if they could show some of my films. Then I slowly found out that I was an honoree. They kind of sneaked it up on me."

Freeman credits part of his success as a film actor to knowing his limitations as a film actor—the fact is, no actor is right for every role; there are characters that are so far afield it stops being a challenge to being lack of self-awareness. In other words, Freeman says, whenever he has found a role difficult, it meant he was in the wrong role.

"I think I'm enough of a technician, as it were, not to have to plumb the depths of my soul. Somebody said, '*You should do Abe Lincoln.*' No, not in a million years would I ever consider doing Abe Lincoln. They say, '*Just do it as an exercise.*' No! It's a travesty."

But when it's a role that fits, Freeman usually makes it a second skin that reels the audience in. "From childhood, I've had the ability to hold your attention—that watch-what-I-can-do thing. It's become part of my arrogance. If I like a character, I think I can always infuse it with some life, some reality. When I fail to do it, I'm crushed. I've been in some turkeys, but critics have been pretty kind about separating me from them."

Sometimes, as Freeman readily admits, he works primarily for the payday. Other times, he works because the character presents a challenge ("A good story and an interesting character is all I am looking for.") or simply because he enjoys acting and prefers not to turn down work. "You can be rejuvenated by going to another job," he says. "Not working is very often dulling."

Then there are times Freeman acts because it's important to him on a personal and social level, such as with *Amistad*. "You may absolutely assume that this is not just another acting job. This is just one of those times when you have a must-do situation, a story that must be told, and if I have the opportunity to be in on the telling, then, yeah, I want to."

Directed by Steven Spielberg, the movie dramatized a little known 1839 revolt aboard the slave ship *Amistad* while it was heading to the Caribbean. A year later the Africans involved were tried in court.

"When I think of things like *Glory* and *Amistad*, these are moments in American history that were completely hidden away," Freeman explains. "There are history buffs who know something about the stories, but the general public knows nothing. I thoroughly believe in the dictum about knowing your history in order to know yourself. As a country, we don't know ourselves. We just know what we've been told in the general history books. I was drawn mostly to the picture itself. You couldn't help but see this was a momentous undertaking in terms of telling the story."

Freeman was cast as abolitionist Theodore Joadson. Anthony Hopkins costarred as President John Quincy Adams, and Djimon Hounsou played legendary rebel Joseph Cinque.

Sengbe Pieh, a father of three and the son of a tribal chief, was a twenty-four-year-old rice farmer in Sierra Leone when he was captured by Spanish slave traders in 1839. Given the name Joseph Cinque by his captors, he was taken to Cuba and sold with forty-seven others as a slave to Jose Ruiz.

Ruiz hired Ramon Ferrer to transport his slaves aboard the *Amistad* to Puerto Pricipe. On July 2, Cinque led an uprising. Ferrer was killed, and the Africans commandeered the ship, directing the navigator to set sail for Africa. But two months later, the *Amistad* was captured off of Long Island by the U.S. Navy. Cinque and the other Africans were jailed in New Haven.

Spain demanded the slaves be returned to Cuba. President Martin van Buren instead ordered the men be tried for murder in America. Defense lawyers Lewis Tappan and James Pennington argued to the court that even though slavery was legal in Cuba, importation of slaves from Africa was not. The judge ruled that indeed the Africans had been illegally kidnapped and as a result had the right to use force to escape from their captors.

The U.S. government appealed the decision to the Supreme Court. Former President John Quincy Adams volunteered to represent the Africans. He delivered a marathon speech before the Justices, who ultimately upheld the Circuit Court judge. Cinque and the surviving Africans were finally returned Sierra Leone, accompanied by five missionaries who established an antislavery mission. In a tragic footnote, Cinque discovered his wife and children had been killed during his absence. He left the mission and his fate remains unknown.

Freeman's Joadson was not a historical character, but a composite representing nineteenth-century black abolitionists. Spielberg was brought the story by producer Debbie Allen, and the first person he sent a script to was Freeman.

"Steven was just adamant that he wanted Morgan Freeman," Allen told the *Washington Post*. "I think if Morgan Freeman wanted to play [the young white attorney] Roger Baldwin, Steven might have found a way," she joked, adding that Freeman's most profound gift is presence.

"I had never seen anyone so powerful, even when he doesn't have anything to say. I watched him dominate scenes where he is just observing. He is kind of like a quiet storm, listening patiently, observing, understanding."

The Freeman-Spielberg admiration society was mutual. Freeman vividly remembers getting the call.

Another one of those moments when your heart goes pitter pat-
ter because I can never explain to you what it's like when the
phone goes and someone says, *"It's for you—it's Steven Spielberg."*

Steven calls up with this incredible script with this really incredible story few people know about. It's such an event in American
history; the fact that it hasn't been told before is amazing.

Here were people who were kidnapped against international
law. What is germane here is that in American courts this law was
held up even though there was slavery in this country. The slave
trade had not been outlawed, yet this was not allowed to continue.

Number one I can't believe the luck, having the sheer luck
at having someone consider me for this wonderful idea. I
really need to knock wood, because part of my career—a large
part of my career—has been enormous amounts of great
good luck. Someone calls me up and says: *"We have this great
project, we thought of you"* . . . *Shawshank Redemption, Se7en,
Amistad, Unforgiven.*

When it's suggested that Freeman's participation might have been
sought to lend a certain credence to the project, he says,

Actually, that's a two-edged sword. In this business, you have
to attach some kind of name to whatever you're working on. So a
lot of us find material coming at us hot and heavy just so someone can say you're interested.

But on something like *Amistad*, I don't think they called me to
lend my weight to it, because you can't get much weightier than
Steven Spielberg. When he calls, I'm already intrigued. It's a place
you want to get to in your career—a sort of first-hired position.

Freeman clearly found joy working with Spielberg.

He's exciting. . . . He knows precisely what he's doing, he's atten-
tive, he's so knowledgeable, he's quick and if you've got an idea,

he's nothing but ears. If you want to say something, you have his total attention. He's all he's cracked up to be.

You know, I have had two really outstanding experiences working on a film. Steven was one. He's in and of himself . . . there's this excitement being around him on the set. Everybody gets it. Clint Eastwood was the other. Just a joy to go make a film with those guys.

Although historical, or costume, dramas were once a staple of Hollywood studios, in recent decades they have been more of a gamble, in part because of skyrocketing production costs—for every *Gladiator* there are expensive bombs like *Barry Lyndon* and *Pearl Harbor*. So it quite often takes someone with the clout of a Spielberg to get such a project greenlit.

It doesn't help matters when an expensive prestige project gets slapped with a messy lawsuit right before its premiere. Prior to *Amistad's* schedule release, author Barbara Chase-Riboud accused Spielberg and his DreamWorks Studio of stealing the story from her book *Echo of Lions*—specifically citing Freeman's character as being plagiarized from the book—and requested an injunction from preventing the film's release.

Producer Debbie Allen said the film was based on the 1974 book *Black Mutiny*, by William Owens, which she optioned. Typically, Freeman took a sage attitude when news of the lawsuit broke.

"DreamWorks will handle it however they handle it. I don't really know what the reason for it is." But he did take issue with a comment made by Chase-Riboud's attorney. The *New York Times* reported the lawyer said, "I don't think there were many wealthy African-Americans living in New England in the 1840s."

Freeman seemed more weary than annoyed by what he clearly perceived as ignorance.

It would be unrealistic to have an abolitionist involved in this without having black representation as a historical footnote. You know what I mean? The amazing thing is that people question the idea of this black man who's got some power and some wealth. They say, "*Was there such a thing?*" You know, I say to them, go study. Find some book. Read it. That's all very correct.

It's not just a black story. It informs America about itself. Those people were Africans, and they weren't slaves. Ultimately, they were seen as . . . freedom fighters.

Chase-Riboud's request for an injunction was denied, and the lawsuit eventually went away. Unfortunately, so did *Amistad* in fairly quick order as it was considered a box office failure. Freeman believes the subject matter hit too close to home for most Americans because slavery "is subject matter that Americans don't want to confront. Americans relate to it the way Germans relate to the Holocaust. So people just didn't want to see it."

He doesn't blame Hollywood, then, for often steering clear of such issues. "The only color in that town is green. Dollar-green, nothing else matters. Hollywood's history is about money, they're not do-gooders. It mirrors society and tries to give society what it will pay for."

Nor will Freeman entertain the criticism, most notably from director Spike Lee, that Spielberg patronized slavery or that black stories are best told by black artists. "That's the race card," Freeman says. "It's something you pull out of your sleeve to create some dialogue or controversy or something. I have no interest in that conversation at all. I don't agree with it, I don't believe in it. What Steven did was make a wonderful movie about American history. And that's as far as that goes."

Despite its lack of commercial success, Freeman is proud of *Amistad*.

I loved the film. I had a moment of err, during the killings. I thought that was a little over-wrought. But [Spielberg] wanted to make a point and I understood that . . . that's what any storyteller wants to do. You're telling it for a purpose; you want to do something to your audience, particularly if you're Steven Spielberg, that's why he's Steven Spielberg. When I walk out of a Steven

Spielberg movie, something has happened to me. When I saw *Close Encounters*, my wife and I jumped into the car and drove out into the country where there were no lights so we could look up and see.

Let me just say this: I love him. I'm at his beck and call—any time of the day or night.

Freeman, however, was becoming much less inclined to heed the call of Broadway anymore.

The whole thing was that eventually I would go back to the stage and do *Lear*. Everyone would say to me that that's what I should do; it'd be a great swansong for me. I hope they meant on the stage—that's pretty ominous. But that was a long time ago, no longer, not interested.

I really do like making movies, and the last time I was onstage, doing *Taming of the Shrew*, (in 1990) I found myself feeling put upon. You've got to rehearse every day for four or five weeks and then you've got to get up onstage and do the same thing.

You do a play and if it's a hit you can stay for years. I like change, I like moving. What I like about film is that you do it and then you move on.

And now over sixty years old, Freeman still showed no signs of slowing down.

To the casual observer, *Se7en's* Detective Somerset may not have seemed all that distinct from *Kiss the Girl's* Detective Alex Cross. Just don't suggest that to Morgan Freeman. "If they say that to me and it's true, then I have really hit bottom. I don't think it's the same guy. The man in *Se7en* was old and jaded and all burned-out. Alex Cross is a younger guy, ambitious . . . and is go-go-go, all over the place. The genre's the same, but the roles are totally different, which is the main thing that I look at."

Freeman says he always goes by what the writer has given him in the script and by that standard, Alex Cross is a unique individual.

What's the background of the average policeman? Some college, usually, followed by the police academy. But here was a guy who had finished college, gone to the police academy, then gone back and gotten a masters and a doctorate. That's some heavy education. Then he writes best-selling books, makes a lot of money and drives a Porsche.

Acting is merely an interpretive endeavor. I don't create anything. I always have to have something to go by. I always have to have very strong input from someone else, who has done the creating. The writer creates; the person who has the idea and sits down and puts it on the blank piece of paper—that's the creator. . . . I take that off the page. If I created the character, it *would* be the same person every time out.

Kiss the Girls is based on James Patterson's best-selling novel, featuring forensic psychologist Dr. Alex Cross who is tracking down a sexual psychopath serial killer who calls himself Casanova. Casanova has abducted eight women, including Cross's niece. Helping him is Kate McTiernan, a surgical intern who managed to escape from Casanova. Cross must race the clock to figure out Casanova's identity before he kills the women he has abducted.

The film's director, Gary Fleder, toned down the book's violence considerably, explaining to the *Daily News* that he preferred to leave it to the audience's imagination.

The book is pretty intense and it would have been way too easy to exploit its violence. I felt like, how much further can American cinema go with corpses and decapitations and viscera? I think that we're inured to that. I felt that I could make a film that was portentous and terrifying and unnerving without being overtly offensive in terms of being gratuitous.

One shot, one scene, one line in the wrong direction and the film could have been misogynist, in my estimation. But I knew that if I just underscored Morgan's and Ashley's characters' points of view, and not support the point of view of the killer, I'd be fine.

You know what? It's so easy to have torture scenes and rape scenes on film. There's no art in that, man. The art is—and I constantly go back to this—like *Jaws*, my favorite film when I was a kid.

The first hour of *Jaws* you don't see the shark, yet you feel completely terrified by this huge monster out there. In fact, when you finally see the thing, it looks like a rubber shark and you're not really scared of it.

Ashley Judd, who costars as Kate and who comes from a family that is openly religious, had to field questions on how she reconciled her spiritual values with a story that was so inherently dark. To Judd, the two are not mutually exclusive.

"It's a really interesting discourse," she acknowledged in an interview with Bob Strauss.

> I think of C. S. Lewis, who wrote *The Screwtape Letters*. This was a man of unimpeachable credentials and obviously devoted Christian morality, and he writes a book from the devil's point of view.
>
> I sort of look at my characters as either having the love of God or not, and I go from there. You know, you don't know what good is unless you can define it by its opposite, and as it says in *The Prophet*, the place that is carved out by your pain is the same vessel in which you feel your joy.
>
> Now, I don't expect people in Keokuk to think about that when they go see me in a movie. But it is important to me.

So was the script's handling of the material.

"The screenplay wasn't prurient," Judd told Strauss. "I read the book when I was screen-testing and it was so much more nasty than the script. And Morgan Freeman is the ultimate bastion of dignity, so I never worried about it for a second."

In fact, Judd and Freeman became fast friends during the shoot after she asked for his help with a personal problem.

"The pivotal moment was when I was getting a little harassed by a certain person on the set of *Kiss the Girls*," Judd recounted to the Los Angeles *Daily News*.

> I was trying to figure out how to handle it, and I decided to go to Morgan for advice. I might have even asked my agent what I

should do, and she said, "*He's your elder, but he's also your colleague and your peer. You guys are sharing this work environment, so ask him.*"

So I went over and said, "*Mr. Morgan, when you have a free moment, there's something I need to ask you.*" And it was like he sprouted these wings. . . . I remember feeling like he puffed up and became this beautiful, encompassing being who enfolded me into his care and confidence. It happened right next to camera, even, and he still sort of shielded me. He tilted his head down with great confidentiality, I poured my heart out and he gave me his impeccable advice. For me, that was really it. I had to work up the courage to approach him in that way, but his response was so welcoming and loving that that helped me segue into believing that, yeah, this guy is my friend.

Freeman acknowledges he shares a unique bond with Judd. "I don't keep in touch with that many people, and we keep in touch. The only other person I keep in touch with is . . . there is nobody! Her sense of humor is one of the more endearing qualities about her, among the many. This playful, kind of kittenish thing she can do . . . and she doesn't take herself too seriously. That makes her special, because I think young, pretty women are driven to that. There may be a fairly high level of intelligence on my end; there's an extraordinary intelligence on her end. I find her intelligence intimidating; she's really, really bright."

Considering his fondness for Judd, it's interesting to hear Freeman say he did not find the experience of shooting *Kiss the Girls* a particularly enjoyable one—although he is quick to give the director kudos. "Gary Fleder is a young man but he has a real flair for making movies. I like working with directors because I'm really opinionated as you might, or might not have gathered by now, about what things work and may not work, what audiences like and may not like. . . . I like to be able to say them and then have them acted on. The director who responds to me like that, always gets my appreciation. I do appreciate it. What I find is the best directors, no matter what kind of name they have, are like that."

In this case, the chemistry worked. *Kiss the Girls* was an unqualified box office hit and was the number one movie in the country for the first two weeks of its release. Morgan Freeman wasn't just a respected actor, he was now considered to be a *bankable* actor, one who could "open" a movie. It's a noticeable achievement for any actor, much less a black actor eligible for AARP, especially when someone like Sidney Poitier puts it in perspective.

"I come from a time when it was an event to see a black person on television," Poitier reminded journalists during a press event in Los Angeles. "I come from a time when it was an event to see a black person on the screen or in the theater, in a role that was not a representation of the stereotypical view of blacks at that time. That's where I come from. I have consequently been around to see the changes."

He also comes from a time when he was essentially the only black actor considered for roles in mainstream movies and says it was relief to finally have some company. "The relief came principally from the fact that I was no longer alone. There came a time when other [black] actors came along: James Earl Jones and Roscoe Lee Brown and Denzel Washington and Wesley Snipes and a good number of others. So it was no longer the lonely journey it had been for so many years."

Casting director and producer Reuben Cannon agreed, telling *Ebony* in a 1997 interview, "I've been in Hollywood for more than twenty years. For a long time when you thought of a Black male star, it was Sidney Poitier, Sidney Poitier, Sidney Poitier. Now we have Morgan, Danny, Laurence Fishburne, Denzel and Wesley. That is indeed progress." He also points out that these actors all happen to be well trained. "They all come out of theater. They have a reservoir of talent."

National Public Radio film critic and host Elvis Mitchell agreed, telling Joy Bennett, "It's rare that [black actors] can just go right into the movie business. In the case of Will Smith or Martin Lawrence, they became famous in other avenues and then went into the movie business. You have to work twice as hard to get half as far—that still applies to show business. Look at Danny Glover and Morgan Freeman. These guys have done a lot of work. By the time they got the chance to be movie stars, they were ready for it."

And they got opportunities Poiter never did. Film historian Donald Bogle told the *Washington Post's* Jacqueline Trescott, "Morgan Freeman has an edge that Sidney doesn't. And Morgan is now a bigger star than Sidney was. . . . His success is a cultural phenomenon at his age."

Typically, Freeman shies away from framing the issue solely in black and white.

> You get some roles because you're Black, and then you get some roles because you can do it. But you try to push toward the idea of open casting in Hollywood. I know independent filmmakers are more receptive to that idea. There's an effort to show that we're a much more diverse society.
>
> This is where we are . . . and we can just go on now and do this. When I read (the novel) *Hawaii*, it said the Chinese had this term for America, called it the Golden Mountain. And I look now at a lot of young people, and the thing that distinguishes them as Americans is this kind of golden color, from all of the races coming together.

The next step is consolidating the increased power black performers are enjoying. "If you want studio power and a piece of the pie, you go build your own studio. You don't sit around waiting for somebody to hand it to you."

Heeding his own advice, Freeman's next feature film was a labor of love called *Under Suspicion*, which he executive produced himself through Revelations Entertainment and costarred opposite good friend Gene Hackman. Intense and gritty, the movie pits Freeman's police detective against Hackman's suspected serial killer. The action takes place over the course of one night when the detective interrogates the prime suspect.

Freeman says he got involved in the project by serendipity. He was at the Four Seasons Hotel in Los Angeles when he ran into Gene Hackman.

"I bumped into Gene in the lobby, and he told me he had this project he was interested in and that he had a tape he wanted to show me."

The tape was a video of Claude Miller's 1981 film *Garde à Vue*, which Hackman had been trying to do as an American remake for twelve years by that time. "We talked later and he asked me if I was interested, and I said yes, and then he asked which part I wanted to play. I told him, '*Oh, I wanted to play the detective*,' and he said that's good because he wanted to play the lawyer. Sometimes it works out."

When Freeman watched the original film, he says he was "very excited, because what I thought . . . I was watching a play. Primarily, these actors are in a stage setting that has nothing else to distract them. Just the human integration, and that's very exciting."

So Revelation Entertainment produced it—*Under Suspicion* was the company's first feature—and Stephen Hopkins was hired to direct the taut script.

"I think that the great unsung heroes of movies are the writers," Freeman says. "If it's not on the page, you're not likely to get it, not so that your audience likes it. . . . And the hardest thing to do is to tell people who are sitting in some of these front offices, *Audiences think, stupid. You can trust that they think.* A lot . . . think that you've got to be spoon fed every little want, every little thing. I don't think that either. You know why I don't think that? Because I am in the audience; I go to movies too."

Freeman says that's why it's easier to get a $150 million film made than a $15 million one.

"I think that the mogul business of people who make these decisions kind of understand that if you have a large budget, not the word blockbuster, but it's a large movie, it's got lots of mayhem and action and stuff like that. Your audience is going to be young and pretty much non-discriminating. They'll be there. Whereas if you do something where you need a thinking audience then you don't have a guarantee."

Although raising the money for *Under Suspicion* was a headache, Freeman's favorite part was working with a man he readily admits is an acting idol. "Working with Gene Hackman was the main draw of this. The project you can almost say is a two-character drama. . . . The other characters are there, but the main cluster of this whole thing is the combat between these two. And having such a theatrical piece to do with someone like Gene Hackman, you do it. Working with peers and real professionals is almost always the same—the underlying factor is trust. Very seldom have I run into an actor who disappointed me."

Despite differing philosophies on technique—Hackman is a Method actor through and through—Freeman says they still clicked.

> Wherever he goes with what he does, he's totally focused on what he's doing. He's not commenting on it, he's not grandstanding with it, he's just focusing on being the deepest and best he can be. And that helps you be the deepest and the best you can be. An actor who's going to run towards the cliff, hold his nose and jump—just hold hands and do it.
>
> This was a very intense piece. . . . The challenge in situations like that is to carry your weight. Gene's at the crux of the emotional impact of this piece; he's the one taking the hard fall, the heavy line. So, the question for me was how successful was I going to be in bringing out the emotional baggage I needed to, because both characters have it.

While the script may have been intense, the atmosphere on the San Juan, Puerto Rico, set was anything but. And for other young actors, it was a unique learning experience.

"Working with these guys was like sword-fighting with Jedi masters," Thomas Jane, who played the detective's assistant, said in a *Daily News* interview. "But Gene and Morgan are two very different actors in terms of style. Hackman is a real logical guy, into very detailed analysis of the truism that action equals character. And Morgan . . . took a lot of naps."

"Between shots, yeah, I just chill," Freeman acknowledges. "I go into my trailer, put my feet up and close my eyes and in no time I'm asleep. Acting is not like being in an office. You don't have to do busy work. I'm on my own until they send for me."

Jane says even on the set, Freeman is "very relaxed, a highly intuitive actor. . . . He keeps it so simple; it's just beautiful."

"I'm a joyous worker," Freeman says. "I have an awful lot of fun, doing one thing or another. But I don't really know a lot about how it works. Intellectualizing about the choices you make and how you get them in terms of acting is really just a lot of bull. I just find it all, usually, so easy to do that I don't know what the mechanisms are."

But Freeman does know what he likes in a director and was complimentary toward director Stephen Hopkins. His greatest asset seemed to be staying out of his star's way. "You can say to me, 'Morgan, wait. Don't say that line until I get this far around so that I can get that light on this side of your face.' I understand it very clearly and I will do as many takes as you want to do to get it just the way you want it. Make sure I understand and it's no problem. Hopkins is like that. He's one of those who sits down and says, 'The way I see it is like this' . . . and every once and awhile he'll say, 'Just step around a little bit more'—that's a technical thing. Simple." But Freeman adds pointedly, "Directors who want to direct actors are headed for trouble. I don't like to be directed. If you cast it right, you just hire someone to say 'Action.' They come in later and say, 'Cut.'"

Under Suspicion was unusual in that many of the scenes were shot in long takes, up to seven minutes in length. "Normally, if you're doing a film with some special effects, you shoot very short segments," Freeman explains.

You very seldom have to learn a page of dialogue. An actor's talent, if they have any at all, is for memory. I can't remember names, but I can look at a page of dialogue and do it.

Because *Under Suspicion* is essentially a play, they didn't need a lot of cuts. There are a lot of close-ups in films by people who've done television. Small screens seem to demand that immediacy, whereas a film doesn't; a film can sustain a tableau. If you have a scene that you can choreograph as a tableau so that the scene is seamless; then, number one, you're going to save time and time is money; and number two, you're going to be more immediate in your story without a lot of jumps and things.

The movie was screened at the Cannes International Film Festival in 2000 and was praised by Claude Miller, who announced it was a better film than his. Freeman says he was flattered—and dubious. "I don't think it's a better film, personally. I think it's a different film. I have a big thing about remakes. I don't think they're worth anything unless you give them something new, unless you make them different. Otherwise, it's just another pillaging of French cinema by Hollywood hacks."

Although well received in Europe, American critics were uniformly negative. The *Dallas Morning News* was representative when it noted,

> *Under Suspicion* has the makings of a first-rate drama: It features two of America's greatest actors, has a compelling premise and deals with moral ambiguity in a sophisticated way. Yet, it's never as good as it should be, with occasional moments of brilliance overshadowed by the gimmicky direction of Stephen Hopkins. . . .
>
> In the end, *Under Suspicion* lacks the sizzle of the original film on which it was based. . . . Mr. Hackman and Mr. Freeman strive mightily to rescue the proceedings. But they can't overcome the misdirection—and poor pacing—of Mr. Hopkins.

The *New York Times's* Elvis Mitchell felt French cinematic sensibilities simply didn't translate to American audiences.

> There's . . . an implicit lack of trust in the audience's interest in minimal dramas and in the actors' abilities to make them work. Swimming against this tide might be one of the things Mr. Hackman found attractive about *Garde* and impelled him to find a way to get it to the United States market. This is an admirable motive, and it's about all *Suspicion* has going for it. . . .
>
> Mr. Hopkins falls victim to the corny misconception of opening up a stagy piece by giving the characters elbow room within the large sets. . . .
>
> Even after the surprise ending—which isn't much of a surprise to anybody, although the two leads invest a great deal of

energy in trying to stave off the plodding and inevitable denouement—the sleaziness of the alleged crime makes *Suspicion* too pat a conceit; there's not much to be suspicious of.

The film's U.S. distributor, Lion's Gate, opened the film in New York and Los Angeles—and nowhere else. Then–Lion's Gate copresident Mark Urman defended the decision to the *Chicago Tribune*. "It really is very expensive to distribute movies, and the marketplace is very crowded, and if a movie does not seem to be commercially viable, you can spend all of that money and end up awash in red ink. Names are not enough. You can spend $15–20 million to get a good opening weekend, and that could be a $12 million weekend."

Taking his usual philosophical approach to life's disappointments, Freeman says just because it's someone's pet project doesn't mean it will be successful. "It happens to all of us."

But it wouldn't stop him from pushing to get his own pet projects made.

13

O N THE EVENING of July 17, 1944, the merchant ship *SS E. A. Bryan* was being loaded with ammunition at Port Chicago, California, located thirty-six miles north of San Francisco near Concord. At the time, the Navy did not allow black servicemen to participate in combat so the job of loading over 4,000 tons of ammunition was assigned to the mostly 1,400 black enlisted men stationed at Port Chicago. In addition to the 320 men working on the pier, there were railcars filled with an additional 429 tons of munitions.

Witnesses later reported that at around 10:20 PM a bright flash streaked into the sky, followed by several small blasts. Then an enormous, thundering explosion cracked the night as the *SS E. A. Bryan* detonated.

According to the Naval Historical Center's Web site, "The seismic shock wave was felt as far away as Boulder City, Nevada. The *E. A. Bryan* and the structures around the pier were completely disintegrated. A pillar of fire and smoke stretched over two miles into the sky above Port Chicago. The largest remaining pieces of the 7,200-ton ship were the size of a suitcase. A plane flying at 9,000 feet reported seeing chunks of white hot metal as big as a house flying past. The shattered *Quinault Victory* was spun into the air. Witnesses reported seeing a 200-foot column on which rode the bow of the ship, its mast still attached. Its remains crashed back into the bay 500 feet away."

The blast left a crater 700 feet long, 300 feet wide, and 66 feet deep. Everyone within 1000 feet of the dock was killed: 320 men in all, 202 of them black—a stunning 15 percent of all black casualties suffered during the whole of World War II.

The Navy moved quickly to determine the cause of the explosion, but a Naval Court failed to ever officially establish what set off the blast. Some speculation was that the volatile explosives used in torpedoes may have been the culprit. Others believe a crane, which had earlier failed a brake inspection, drop a load of ammunition on the dock. That would have caused the first smaller series of explosions, which detonated the ammo on the ship.

While the all-white court cleared the white officers, it tacitly damned the black victims, concluding the black sailors who had been loading the ship "are neither intellectually nor temperamentally capable of handling high explosives."

Not addressed were the repeated complaints from the men about lack of training and unsafe conditions for loading ammunition—concerns that were ignored by the white officers.

Initially, the black enlisted men stationed at Port Chicago were given other duties but on August 9, three hundred of the men were assigned to the Mare Island Naval facility for ammunition duty. This time, the majority refused, claiming that they had never been properly trained and that there the same unsafe conditions at Mare Island as there had been at Port Chicago.

Two hundred and fifty men were jailed for three days, threatened with mutiny charges—a crime punishable by death in times of war. Two hundred of the men relented, but fifty black enlisted men didn't. Rather than the lesser charge of disobeying an order, they were charged with mutiny and ordered to stand trial.

Freeman admits he was ignorant of the salient facts of the Port

Chicago disaster. "I knew there was a massive explosion somewhere in the U.S. during World War II. I didn't know Port Chicago was in California."

But he took a crash course after he says NBC offered him the chance to produce a made-for-television movie based on the Port Chicago mutiny. It was a project he couldn't turn down, and once again Morgan found himself helping give America a history lesson. "This country was built by an awfully large array of people with culturally diverse backgrounds whose history and participation (have) largely been neglected. Anytime I can come across material that helps fill in those gaps, that's what I want to do."

He admits, "I know that I am informed about history through books and movies. You can teach me more if I have some concept, having seen it in the movies or read about it in a book, than you can if I have not. The danger is always that in Hollywood we tend to rewrite history to match what we need to say, which means that it's no longer history, it's somebody's fiction. But pictures like *Glory*, where we strove mightily to be accurate, I think are important and I like to do those."

Mutiny was also such a project. Freeman compared its importance to films like *Glory* and *Amistad* because it "tells of moments in American history that were hidden. History buffs know about these stories, but the general public knows nothing. I strongly believe you must know your history in order to know yourself. We just know what we've been told in the history books. Nobody knows anything about this incident or black involvement in the war, especially people who've studied World War II.

"Since the Emancipation Proclamation black people have been praying and hoping and fighting for total inclusion. Every time a war comes along, here's a shot! We'd join right up. Afterwards—until Vietnam—no matter what the courage quotient, we were disarmed."

As such, it makes nostalgic reminisces of The Best Generation ring a little hollow for Freeman. "What criteria are you going to use to say that was the best generation? Is that a generalized statement or does it include all of us? If it includes all of us, then that statement's wrong, because this is institutionalized exclusion. It behooves us to try and tell the stories that have been neglected."

The telefilm follows the story through the court martial, where after thirty-two days of testimony, it took less than an hour and a half of deliberation by the court to find all the men guilty and sentence them to fifteen years' hard labor in prison. They were also given dishonorable discharges.

"It is a case with many shades of gray," says Freeman. "I would hope the movie would spark dialogue. I don't think anyone is going to say the Navy or the men were 100 percent wrong. But there is more against the Navy."

They were treated like workhorses, like mules. They were taking undue risks in handling munitions without proper training. They were not even allowed to use restrooms on the dock. They had to walk up to a mile to get to the colored-only restrooms.

These men stood up for their rights, with some dignity. They stood like men instead of lying down and being whupped like dogs. The Navy made examples of them, on the theory that someone had to pay. The Navy called it mutiny—but was it really? Perhaps the white commanders were at fault. Whatever, they went after the black men under color of authority.

The movie was shot without the cooperation of the Navy, primarily because nobody asked them. The film shot on location at closed naval bases and used an old World War II–era ship called the *Tulane Victory* to stand in for the *E. A. Bryan*.

The script was based on court transcripts and interviews with survivors who had been stationed at Port Chicago, although the characters are composites of the real servicemen. "There were just too many people to deal with and if you used one guy's name you had to use all the names," Freeman explains. "We had to narrow the focus down. We had to do it this way." But he adds, "The survivors are the most amazing group of people you ever met. As patriotic as any ex-servicemen anywhere under any circumstances and you get no sense of bitterness from these men."

The only historical figure in *Mutiny* is Thurgood Marshall, who at the time was chief counsel for the NAACP. Although he could not directly defend the fifty men because it was a military court martial, Marshall, who would later serve on the Supreme Court, filed a brief with the court in defense of the men. Part of the brief reads, "Negroes in the Navy don't mind loading ammunition. They just want to know why they are the only ones doing the loading!"

Although nobody knew for sure, as far as could be discerned only a couple of the convicted men were still alive at the time of the shoot. It was speculated than many might have changed their names out of disgrace, or in an effort to get a job.

In 1946, President Truman pardoned the men still in prison. Over the years there have been several calls for the Navy to overturn the convictions, but as recently as 1994, it was determined the men received a fair trial and upheld the sentences.

David Ramsey, who appeared in *Mutiny*, feels the men, living or dead, deserve a fresh look at their case. "There's a real human element to the story. These were men with great honor and dignity who went to war for this country. At a minimum, I think the case should be reopened. But it's going to take more than a TV movie to do it."

Freeman agrees. "It's now history, and time (for it) to be dealt with, so we can close the books on it. We all know that history is very selective. It's like talking about the internship of the Japanese-Americans in the war—it's part of what we did. On the one hand, I don't think we should dwell on all the tragedies we have perpetrated against ourselves. "But . . . if you don't understand history, you're doomed to repeat it."

Even though he did not appear in the telefilm, the heavy emotion of the project left Freeman craving something on the light side. "I'm drawn to these things," he admits, "but I'm drawn to these other roles that don't quite have that gravitas."

The decidedly dark comedy *Nurse Betty* was just what the doctor ordered. Freeman plays Charlie, a hit man on the verge of retirement who falls in love with his delusional intended last victim—a waitress from Kansas suffering from posttraumatic amnesia, who thinks she's a character in a soap opera and heads to Hollywood in pursuit of a handsome soap star she has a crush on.

"The only thing that attracts me about any group of roles is their difference," he explains. "The joy, of course, in acting is to be as many different people as you can, and the even greater joy is to be as many different people as you can in the shortest possible time. That's why actors enjoy repertory theater so much. You know, we all want to hide; I don't want to be me in any role at all. The more obfuscation I can find for this Morgan Freeman, the better."

It was his first film role in over a year; after making four films back to back, he spent most of 1998 sailing while intentionally lowering his profile. "I was on hiatus, and I wasn't," he says. "I felt I was too much in the public's face. I thought I'd back away from the public before they backed away from me."

While on his boat cruising the Caribbean, Freeman says he was completely isolated and unreachable. "I dropped off the edge of the Earth. At sea, I really depend on me. When it's rough and ugly or even scary and terrifying, all the other things drop away."

Feeling refreshed and anxious to get back to work, *Nurse Betty* was just the challenge Freeman needed. "This is one of those cases when you say, *okay, I've seen this and I've seen this,* but together you have not. At no time can you be able to predict what's coming next in this movie. As for the character himself, he takes this incredibly bizarre path through the picture. It's such a sly, slow transformation he has; it was just one of those things where, given the chance to pull it off, you have to see if you can do it."

Perhaps most surprising for Freeman is that he was working with director Neil LaBute.

I saw his first movie, *In the Company of Men,* and I thought it sucked deeply. I mean, talk about a couple of scuzzy guys. Man, they were turds. But I was intrigued by the mind that would think this up and film it.

Then I saw LaBute's second movie, *Your Friends & Neighbors*. Not any better, but still intriguing. . . . So then I got the script for *Nurse Betty*, and I loved it and I went and met him. And it turns out he's married, has these lovely kids. He's just this big bear of a man. Cuddly, even. It didn't take any persuading to convince me to do the film.

The same would not be true of his next role because for the first time in his career, Freeman would be asked to reprise a role. And he would break one of his own cardinal rules by accepting.

At least Morgan Freeman is an honest man. For years it had almost seemed a point of honor to him that he was always doing a new character, exploring new ground, but when he was offered the chance to reprise his role as Dr. Alex Cross in *Along Came a Spider*, he accepted, for a number of reasons.

"You might imagine that I got paid well," he says. "And it's really not a bad character. And at home, you've got two offices and a house full of people telling me that I ought to do it."

Never one to mince words, Freeman does readily admit that "Alex is not my favorite role. And, yes, I'm very suspicious of doing a role as a franchise. Probably the only one that held up that well is James Bond, and Alex is no James Bond." That said, he adds, "I like Alex because he's more cerebral than active. His particular strength is as a mind hunter. I like playing that."

James Patterson, who authors the Alex Cross mystery series, said Freeman wasn't exactly his vision of Dr. Cross. "I had someone like Muhammad Ali in mind," Patterson said in a *Virginian-Pilot* interview when the film was released. But he was quick to add, "Morgan is an actor who rises above everyone, like Michael Jordan in a basketball game. . . . There is one thing I regret—they never let Morgan break loose. On the set, he laughs. He has emotions. In the film, he plays Alex as very quiet. Very thoughtful."

Most significantly, the movie steers clear of an interracial romance Cross had in the novel with his female partner. The film's director, Lee Tamahori, defended the decision to Mal Vincent, saying the decision wasn't made for "any racial reasons. It was because of age. Monica is younger than the character in the novel and Morgan is older. A romance would have looked silly and might even have made Alex Cross look dumb. It wasn't needed for the plot. In fact, it wasn't appropriate for the plot."

In addition to starring in the film, Freeman was also an executive producer through Revelations Entertainment, which coproduced the film. *Entertainment Weekly* reported that the shoot was difficult, saying, "Freeman was openly critical of the script's frailties while shooting the picture, especially the ending, which was rewritten and reshot a half-dozen times."

Because he had played the character before, the second film needed to stay true to the character he had created in *Kiss the Girls*. "You know what kind of moves [Cross] would make, mentally," he explained to Benjamin Svetkey. "You know what kind of thought processes he is set to go through. And if things don't seem to go along that line, you have to say, *Wait, wait, wait, wait. This is not the right guy. You're not making the right moves here.*"

Along Came a Spider was modestly successful, earning $74 million in domestic box office and giving Freeman yet another feather in his creative cap. But he worked so much it seemed as if he always had several new films under his belt by the time any of his movies were released. Since none of his films were shot in Mississippi, it meant Freeman was racking up the frequent flier miles.

The demands of making a movie often left little time for sightseeing. "We're always seeing places but a lot of the places we see we don't see much of. . . . You get to your hotel, you go to bed, you get up at 5:00 in the morning, you get in the car and you go to the set, you work until nightfall and get back in the car and go back to the hotel . . . and go to bed. You get one day off and I'm not a big sightseer."

But even if he didn't get to play tourist, the work environment offered by some cities left fond memories—or not. "Some places you been before are so great that you don't ever mind going back. Some places you been before you don't ever want to go back, you know, like Montreal in the winter."

The warmth of the South was much more to Freeman's liking, as was its character. "It keeps us both grounded," Freeman says of he and his wife's Mississippi home. "When we're away from Mississippi for an extended period of time, we enjoy coming home. Myrna and I will walk back and forth through our house, just enjoying it, or I'll ride one of my horses around our property. This is really a lovely place."

His ranch is off a two-lane road about forty minutes outside of Clarksdale. Atop the wrought iron gate leading into his property is the word SONEDNA.

"Those were my parents," he explains, referring to Mayme Edna and Grafton "Son" Curtis, his mother and stepfather. Although his parents were poor most of their lives, they loved their piece of heaven. So it was the place Freeman wanted to give back to. He quietly established the Rock River Foundation, which provides funding to nonprofits promoting culture and arts education as well as matching individual scholarships and grants for Mississippi schoolchildren.

"Once you get something like this started, it's a groundswell," Freeman says. "You're not just giving money away, you're involving more people with the same goal: to improve education in Mississippi."

More publicly, Freeman was also becoming a local Clarksdale entrepreneur, which he says is one of the reasons he decided to return home permanently in the 1990s. "One reason to be back here is because I made a lot of money and I am going to spend it somewhere. This is the best place to spend it."

His first experience with local Mississippi was less than sanguine. When he decided to sell his condo in Manhattan and move full time to

Mississippi, Freeman and his wife hired a contractor to build their dream house. Two years later, they were still waiting.

"You could have built a forty-story building in New York faster than we were building our house," Freeman says.

Wanting to give the contractor a legal goose, Freeman retained a Clarksdale attorney they were told specialized in such matters. His name was Bill Luckett and he succeeded in getting the Freemans into their home in November 1998. Bill and Morgan immediately hit it off, finding in each other kindred spirits.

"Morgan is profoundly intelligent and all the other things he seems on screen," Luckett said in an *Atlanta Journal Constitution* interview, "but he's also a lot of fun. We love to raise hell together. We'll go down the highway at 3 o'clock in the morning with the radio blasting and both of us singing at the top of our lungs."

Bill and Morgan, along with their wives, became close friends, frequently traveling to Memphis for a night on the town. When Freeman learned that Luckett was thinking of turning an abandoned storefront into an upscale restaurant in Clarksdale, Morgan wanted in, in part he says, so he wouldn't have to go all the way to Memphis for a four-star meal.

"Bill has renovated numerous houses in and around Clarksdale for years . . . so I knew what he was capable of," Freeman says. "He was already one of the finest businessmen I knew."

So Freeman and Luckett became equal partners in Madidi, named after a Bolivian national park known for its ecological purity. Freeman saw parallels with Mississippi's Delta way of life that has remained, in many ways, pure to itself. Reflecting that unique lifestyle is the restaurant's artwork, which showcases many Mississippi artists.

At Madidi's grand opening in 2001, Freeman used his star power to generate media interest and welcomed guests and media dressed in a formal tuxedo that belies his typical down-home self. Even the governor showed up to offer congratulations and have his picture taken with Freeman. But no doubt his favorite part of the evening was after dinner when everyone ended up at a local juke-joint where Freeman showed off his dance moves.

Like any native Mississippian, Freeman has music in his blood. Most music historians consider Clarksdale ground zero for the blues. Although it only has twenty thousand residents, Clarksdale's hometown talent reads like a Who's Who—Muddy Waters, Ike Turner and Sam Cooke all lived in the area. Most famously, though, its pedigree evolved from legendary bluesman Robert Johnson. According to legend, it was Clarksdale where Johnson sold his soul to the devil in exchange for a guitar.

Freeman says he believes the *essence* of the legend.

You have the devil, and everybody sort of accepts that he is the harbinger or bringer or exemplar of bad times. And the blues is an expression of that. It's letting it out, the way you vent. *If I didn't have bad luck, I'd have no luck as all*—that's the blues.

Legends are always based on reality. Every legend is built on some basic reality. Of necessity, we take some real happening and in order for it to survive, we have to give it weight. And I think that's where this legend comes from. The fact this music survives and that his name survives with that attachment means that it's true.

As far as the real devil? "Well, I'm a bit of Zen follower. I don't really believe in any of that—the devil, etc. But I do believe in balance. If you believe in good, evil exists."

Freeman's sense of history prompted him to suggest he and Luckett open a blues club so that new generations can be exposed to a vital part of Americana. "I think it behoove us, not just African-Americans but Americans, because it is America's own music. You go from the blues all the way up into rock 'n' roll. I spoke to a jazz musician in Los Angeles . . . and he said, '*You know, no blues, no jazz.*' The fact that the music does evolve, we have to accept that. What we need to hold on to is . . . the knowledge that this is important music, and the blues is actually our classic music."

That was fading into oblivion as juke joints across the south were closing. "We were always hearing on the street, *Where can we hear some live blues music?*" Luckett recalls. "No place in town was offering regularly scheduled, consistently played blues music. It was a hit-or-miss thing. . . . So we decided to change that."

They converted a turn-of-the-twentieth-century cotton warehouse into a modern-day juke-joint called Ground Zero that offers live music Wednesday, Friday, and Saturday nights with an occasional Sunday brunch. Located next door to the Delta Blues Museum, the joint's ambience is as different from Madidi as catfish is from sushi. Customers eat at simple tables and sit on folding chairs because the main draw is the music.

"Clarksdale is the crossroads of the blues, and we wanted a place to showcase up-and-comers," says Freeman. "We want to hold onto the basic feel and sensibility of the place," he adds. "We don't want it too high-toned, because the minute you get too big, you become like Beale Street, New Orleans, or any other place that becomes touristy, very surface and commercial. Right now, Clarksdale is very real."

That authenticity is exactly why the city has become a tourist destination. "What we have to give is thanks for is the fact that now there is a music trail that people have discovered and are using," Freeman says. "They start in Nashville. They go to Memphis, Clarksdale and New Orleans, or they'll start in New Orleans and work their way back. And we are actually still considered the center of that and people come from everywhere. It's amazing."

And while Freeman is glad to help bring recognition to the area, there have been drawbacks for him personally. "Sometimes when I am home I get to go to Ground Zero, but I can't stay for very long. Everybody has a camera and bits of paper," to ask for an autograph or have a picture taken.

While the power of his celebrity undeniably benefited his business ventures, it did little to correct what Freeman feels is a long-standing wrong. Shortly before Ground Zero opened, the state of Mississippi voted on a highly emotional, contentious issue—whether states should be represented by images of the Confederate flag and what it inherently stood for.

The current state flag has the Confederate flag in the upper left corner. The proposed new design had red, white, and blue stripes and 20 stars, representing the 13 original colonies, the 6 nations or governments that have curled Mississippi in its history, and one star commemorating being the twentieth state admitted to the union in 1817. The current flag was adopted in 1894.

The flag, the stars and bars, has personal resonance to me because to me it doesn't represent so much the South as a very negative mind-set that is not necessarily southern. You see that flag wherever you see skinheads, radical right wingers, neo-Nazis, any hate group. It throws such a terrible light on the state.

That flag has always represented, number one, treason and, number two, a separation of white people from Jews, niggers and homosexuals. And you can't change that.

That flag and the KKK go together like biscuits and molasses. When I see it, it sends a chill through me. It's a sense memory, like the feeling you get the first time you hit your thumb with a hammer. You never forget it.

Freeman was careful not to lump all those wanting to keep the flag as it was into the same pot. "I know that the bulk of the people who are supporting the [current] flag are not in it for negative reasons. Personally, I have every appreciation for those Mississippians who say the flag represents their heritage. But it's not everybody's heritage. You can't tell me I'm never going to be able to look at that flag and think, *Ah, it's my heritage, my, you know. . . .* Never."

Freeman, who normally avoids getting too political, was in the forefront of the referendum, appearing on radio ads urging fellow Mississippians to approve a new banner. But it was to no avail. On April 17, the measure to change the flag was resoundingly defeated by a two-to-one margin.

"He was very hurt, as was I, over the flag vote, but we both realized it was as much the fault of apathetic black voters as anyone," Luckett said in a Knight-Ridder interview. "Progressive white counties voted to change the flag. A lot of black voters didn't care."

While pollsters indeed reported that participation by black voters was low, Freeman didn't see it as not caring and a more defeatist attitude. "They still feel that they do not have a say. That's why they don't do it. That's the apathy part of it. *It just doesn't matter what I do—it's not going to change anything.* It's too bad."

Freeman was in Montreal filming *The Sum of All Fears* when the vote took place. After hearing the results, he wrote a long e-mail sharing his personal hurt over the outcome.

"Morgan felt slapped in the face," his wife, Myrna Colley-Lee says.

His disappointment forced Freeman to reassess whether it had affected his affection and loyalty to Mississippi. In the end, he determined it didn't. "When I left Mississippi in the fifties, I thought this was the last place on earth I'd want to come back to. But I have. There are some stubborn people in this state," Freeman observes, "but I could never leave. My parents are here. Can't run away from it. All I can do is try to change it."

ALTHOUGH HIS CINEMATIC characters tend to be methodical and cerebral—traits Morgan Freeman certainly shares—there is a side of his personality that rarely gets reflected in his roles, that of outdoorsman. Perhaps it's to balance the endless hours actors spend in their trailers waiting to shoot a scene or the time they spend on windowless soundstages, but when he isn't working, Freeman is engaged in some physical activity whether it be horse riding, working out with weights, sailing, or trying to beat land speed records for local back roads near his home—he admits to reaching 160 mph in his BMW 745. His exasperated wife has complained more than once to reporters that she wished the cops would stop letting Morgan off with warnings and give him an expensive speeding ticket just once.

His love of speed prompted Morgan to accept an invitation to drive the pace car at the Indianapolis 500 in 2004. Freeman took his first spins around the track as a passenger in a car driven by pro driver Johnny Rutherford. Afterward, Freeman told reporters it wasn't like driving in the flatlands of Mississippi.

"Turn one looks impossible," he said. "You're coming off the front straightaway at an incredible rate. And I'm talking about me now, not a seasoned race car driver. I'm talking about a guy who just got into a car on the track and has gotten his speed up to 130, 140 miles an hour, and he's looking down at turn one."

But after taking a few laps around the track on his own and some coaching by Rutherford, a three-time Indy winner, to not jerk the wheel, Freeman was practically ready to suit up for the big race. But he had to be content with giving members of the media rides around the track. "They said, we like to keep it down to about 100 in the turns, so I was up to about 110, 115, . . . By the time I was finished, I was going into turn one at 120," Freeman said.

The pace car typically leads the racers around the track twice, accelerating to around 100 mph before pulling into the pit and letting the race start. "When I come off turn three, that's when my blood pressure is going to be a little high," Freeman said. "If you're going too slow, you might not make it. The guy that's on your left may be coming up that way, so you really do have to be on it coming off of there."

His excitement was almost childlike. "My life has been, is, I should say, a series of dreams coming true and this will largely be another one."

All in keeping with Freeman's philosophy—"Use it or lose it"—so he keeps living life nonstop, working and playing with equal fervor, imbuing him with the energy of a man decades younger. One of his dream projects would allow the lanky six-foot two-inch Freeman to not only show off his acting chops but also his physicality and riding skills.

"There is a character I've been trying to develop a script for: Bass Reeves, a deputy United States marshal back in the 1870s in Oklahoma territory." Reeves was the first black American to be commissioned as a U.S. deputy marshal west of the Mississippi. According to Freeman, Judge Isaac Parker "hired all these deputy marshals—blacks, whites, Indians," to track down outlaws who had escaped into Indian Territory, "and Bass Reeves was one of the best he had.

"Americans don't know about him. Americans' standard feeling is that only whites settled this country and did all the fighting and all the building and inventing and creating, and so we've all grown up with misinformation about who we are. I see opportunities and reasons to change that."

Freeman's next film would tackle subject matter that had suddenly gone from the realm of fiction to the new reality faced by Americans. In *The Sum of All Fears*, Freeman starred as a CIA director dealing with a terrorist crisis, based on the book by Tom Clancy. In today's world, such a scenario is all too real, but when the movie started shooting in early 2001, the idea of the United States being attacked on her own soil was still the stuff of spy novels, so for Freeman the movie started as a lark.

"I'm a fan of [Clancy's] books, and a fan of the movies that were made from his books—all produced by Mace Neufeld, one of our top-notch producers. I just felt like I was in good hands all the way, and I read the script and it was just terrific, offering me a wonderful part to play. It's all about the part."

The film was in postproduction on September 11, 2001, and suddenly the movie's plot—terrorists plot to detonate a nuclear bomb in an American city—had new resonance.

"Studio marketing people all wondered about whether to release or to hold onto movies that had uncomfortable subject matter," Freeman recalls. "The decision was made with *The Sum of All Fears* to wait an appreciable amount of time and see how it would be received by audiences."

Prior to its scheduled release date in 2002, Neufeld held test screenings to gauge whether audiences were ready for a film when the images from September 11 were still so fresh in every American's mind. After he screened the movie for members of Congress, he felt confident they were.

"I was very anxious to see what the response would be, and it was remarkable," he reported to the *Arizona Republic*. "This is a town where they got hit . . . and the attitude here was that this was a picture a lot of people should see, that it was a cautionary tale and it could certainly keep people from becoming complacent."

During the press junket for the film, Freeman was asked if he thought people would stay away, not wanting to be reminded of the terrible day in September. "The concern remains because the press was going to be constantly talking about it and asking the same question, out loud," he observed to Bill Muller. "And even if the public was *not* that concerned, they *will* be concerned."

But in the end, he said, "It's not for me to think—there the movie is. Whether or not the public is ready for it, we're going to find out. I can't imagine that they wouldn't be. I don't want to imagine it. It might upset people more, particularly with the president talking about us getting back into nuclear armaments development. But that we, as Americans, will always be able to question, always be able to challenge—that's a good thing."

When it was time to hand out the Academy Awards in 2002, Morgan Freeman wasn't among the Hollywood notables walking down the red carpet. He watched it at home with his *The Sum of All Fears* director Phil Robinson. Even though he wasn't up for an award, it was still a memorable ceremony and one Freeman and other black actors watched with special interest because for the first time two black actors were competing for best actor—Denzel Washington for *Training Day* and Will Smith for his portray of boxing legend Muhammad Ali in *Ali*. In addition, Halle Berry's performance in *Monster's Ball* earned her a best actress nomination. It was the first time in thirty years that three black actors received best acting nominations; in 1972, Cicely Tyson and Paul Winfield were nominated for *Sounder* along with Diana Ross for *Lady Sings the Blues*.

All lost.

After the nominations were announced, the reaction was surprisingly muted. "It may be a bit premature to get too excited about nominations when there are no clear winners, since people remember the winners and usually forget the nominees," Todd Boyd, a professor of critical studies at the University of Southern California's School of Cinema and Television, explained in the *Boston Globe*. "Three nominations for black actors does not mean Hollywood is any less racist, and it doesn't mean the academy is any more forward-looking in terms of their outlook on race. It simply means three people have been nominated. If any of them win, that's a different conversation. At this point, there have been black nominees before, there have even been black people who have won. But in 2002, the stakes are a lot higher, and people shouldn't be expected to get all excited by three nominations."

In fact, there was the seemingly incongruous concern that such recognition could be a bad thing. According to a *New York Times* interview, then-NAACP president Kweisi Mfume worried that efforts to diversify would ease up because the perception would be that equality in the entertainment industry had been achieved.

"That's a real fear here," said Mfume. "People asked me the other day, *'Is this progress or a net gain?'* And I said, *'It's progress, but it's no net gain.'*" His point being that while performers may be gaining, the ranks of executives and behind the scenes talent were still blindingly white.

Not everyone chose to view the nominations in terms of black and white. Columnist Martin Grove wrote on the *Hollywood Reporter* Web site that even though it could be "analyzed a million and one different ways," what should be celebrated was that those nominated were "three actors who got honored for terrific performances. I don't think anyone honored them because they're African-American, and I don't think anyone would have voted against them for that reason either. They're three terrific actors."

For Freeman, it was all positive. "The industry has out-stripped the country at large but it has always been that way. You usually find it is the most liberal people who come together to make art."

It was also emotional to see Washington and Berry win. "It's a seminal moment for the industry itself," he later said, adding that watching Halle Berry's acceptance speech "was just a tearjerker. I cried right along with her. The whole world did. It means that it can and will be done."

It's not surprising that Freeman has strong feelings about Martin Luther King, who believed the way to equality was through peaceful change. In July 2002, Freeman agreed to donate his services to appear in a series of Public Service Announcements intended to raise public awareness of the effort being made to finance and build a Martin Luther King memorial on the National Mall in Washington, D.C.

In a related online discussion on Washingtonpost.com, Freeman said, "Every aspect of this monument seems appropriate for these times. While some are confused and frustrated today with the conditions of our world, the monument offers the tenets of Christ, as Dr. King understood them, to provide calm. . . . The monument's etched phrases will speak of the peace within one's self. . . . The monument itself—a peace monument to a peaceful man in a valley that has long commemorated great and hard-fought wars and the Presidents of our vast and diverse nation—the very idea of it pulses."

Freeman said that King deeply affected people in the area he grew up.

He was a person, more than any actor, more than just about any other statesman of his time, who had *presence* in the surest form. I believe it was something that was born in him but that he cultivated with resolution because he knew the power that his particular kind of presence could have in the world.

He knew that change was inevitable but that choice affecting change, non-violence affecting change, peace in the midst of change would make the difference. This is a powerful example that he set for us and posterity. Any reminder of the example that was his life is important. In times of war, of heartache, of despair—in the best of times, we need to remember the power of an exemplary life. We need to remember, always, Dr. King's tenets and his life.

Freeman's next project also dealt with themes of change as well as redemption and faith. Produced by Revelations, *Levity* is an artful examination of how to balance the scales of our live. Billy Bob Thorton starred as a convicted murderer released after serving twenty-three years for killing a man during a botched robbery. He has kept a picture of his victim in his cell so that he would not forget the life he took.

For screenwriter Ed Solomon, *Levity* was quite a departure from his big budget hits *Men in Black* and *Bill and Ted's Excellent Adventure* and had its roots in a personal experience. While studying economics at

UCLA, Solomon volunteered to tutor juvenile inmates through a university outreach program. "I worked with a kid who had recently killed somebody, and though he was only there for a few weeks—on his 18th birthday he was transferred to the state prison where he was to spend the rest of his life—he left an indelible image that still haunts me," Solomon recalled to the *Boston Globe*. "He kept a photo of the boy he killed, and he would constantly unfold it, turn it over, refold it, open it again and stare at it. Until the moment that he had pulled the trigger, the boy had been a stranger to him. But now he was never without him . . . two boys, forever bonded by that one horrible deed."

Everyone involved with the film understood it would never be a box office bonanza, but they were willing to work for a fraction of their normal fees to make the personal, thoughtful film—something becoming more and more difficult.

"On a corporate level, it is harder to make any kind of film that's of interest to you," Solomon says. "There are not the channels that there were 25 years ago. Whether it's your favorite bookstore or coffee shop or movie theater, all those pockets of culture are disappearing for a kind of sameness."

Freeman costarred as a preacher who runs the community house where the ex-con comes to stay. Several years earlier he had turned down the script but offered suggestions on how to improve the characters. The next time he was sent the script, he agreed not only to appear in it but also to produce, believing it to be one of those stories that ought to be told.

While society seems to have adopted an attitude that stiffer sentences as opposed to rehabilitation is the answer, the film offers a different viewpoint. "A little while back there was a woman who was on trial for having murdered her son," Freeman says. "It wasn't really a murder; it was a mercy killing because he had one of those terrible, terrible diseases. She'd seen her husband die of it. . . . [Her son] was in the hospital, looking at her like, *Momma, I can't*. So I wouldn't even put that woman on trial because she's gonna pay, she's gonna pay. She did that out of all of the love that a mother could muster. I can't imagine what it takes to kill your own child. If she says, *Put me in jail* . . . I'll put you in jail, but you don't need to go. You're going to make yourself pay. It's the same thing with this guy. He was a kid and he never forgave himself and he needed someone else to say, *It's all right, you're forgiven.*"

Although he's listed as executive producer, Freeman is quick to admit he did nothing in particular to earn the title. "Let me tell you about being executive producer. It is not a job, it's a title. Don't go around asking executive producers what they do because they don't do anything, all right? In my case, I'm involved from the standpoint that my company is involved in the development. My partner [Lori McCreary] is a producer and she does the hard work. I just get the credit."

And the frostbite. The movie filmed in Montreal during the winter, a misery for Freeman. "If you're like me, a person who really detests cold, it's hard to work in those conditions. You can't get me warm if you get me outside. You can stuff me with all kinds of clothes and pour hot soup all over me, I'm cold and I don't like it, and you can't make me like it."

The warm-blooded actor found himself shivering through the Canadian locations for *Dreamcatcher* as well. When someone suggested a hot toddy or nip from a flask might help, Freeman laughed and declined. "Let me be the first to tell you, drinking alcohol is the worst thing to do in cold weather. Hot soup is the best because the process of digesting food helps to warm you up. I know all of that, and it works for some people, not for me. I don't know how I cope. I just do the best that I can and sometimes I get sick and that gets me in bed and I can stay put for a while."

The upside of *Dreamcatcher* was that Morgan got to play a murderous military man tracking eel-like alien parasites. In his exuberance, he slaughters an entire town trying to keep the parasites contained. "Something comes along every now and then that allows you to let your dark side shine through a little bit—and it's fun," Freeman laughs.

Freeman came up with the character's bushy white eyebrows and wild mass of hair. "I never wanted to play him over-the-top, but I did want the fact that he is a bizarre personality to be clear," Freeman explains. "When you see him coming, you say, *Oh my god. What . . . the . . . heck?*"

Again, Freeman had no illusions about the film's place in the pantheon of his career. "The critics have already trashed it," he said shortly after the film was released, "but I think the kids will like it."

More on his mind was that he was between jobs, telling reporter Moira Macdonald. "I'm looking for work."

While art is important to Freeman, the days of poverty are never that far behind him and making money remains a prime motivator.

It guarantees that I pay my rent. One more year! I have to worry. Everything is relative. So if you gotta live on a dollar, you live on a dollar. I do worry about rent. Rent on the house, the boat, the car and the office. So you gotta think rent. But the best part of anything is knowing you want to do it and getting it.

If something comes along that interests you for whatever reason, and there are at least three that I can think of, money being one, a good script being two, or an outstanding or an interesting cast being three. You're not going to work that often—I don't care what—so you just keep going because sooner or later, and you don't know whether it's going to be sooner, or later, but the phone stops ringing.

So when the accolades come, Freeman makes sure to enjoy the moment. On March 18, 2003, Freeman received a star on Hollywood's Walk of Fame. When asked what the honor meant, Freeman said, "Someone on the day of . . . said, 'You've probably been waiting all of your life for this.' I said, 'Truthfully, no. This isn't something that you wait for. This is a gift.' Having a star on the Walk of Fame, it's one of those acknowledgments that you are where you belong. Welcome to the Pantheon, people have gotten here and stayed a minute longer than fifteen. It feels good, it feels very good."

At the same time, he wasn't completely comfortable racking up the life achievement awards just yet, such as the Mayor's Lifetime Achievement Award at Denver International Film Festival in 2004.

"Seems like a lot of people want to give me achievement awards, but

I'm balking," Freeman said prior to the event. "I've prevailed upon someone to call it something else . . . like an encouragement award. I'm just hitting my real stride here. I haven't really achieved anything yet. I'm just doing life. I'm not looking back yet. I'm not quantifying. Every now and then you do look back and see where you've come from, but it's hard to think of life achievement when life is still going on."

Especially when that life was so full. While filming *The Big Bounce* in Hawaii, Freeman pursued his latest expensive hobby—learning to fly, finally fulfilling a lifelong dream at sixty-five. "I was a student pilot trying to get my instrument rating, so I went to flight school in Hawaii and worked with a really terrific guy there."

Now Freeman can pilot himself to the Caribbean when the urge to go sailing strikes him or fly cross country to a movie location. But unlike the local cops who for years have let him get away with speeding, the FAA proved decidedly stricter when Freeman failed to adhere to procedure, temporarily grounding him in 2004.

"I was flying into Teterboro [New Jersey] on a very busy day. I was at 3,000 feet, having come down from 21,000 feet. Looking at the approach plates, I thought I was supposed to be at 2,000 feet, so I descended to that altitude on my own. But you don't go to certain altitudes till you're told. The control tower said, *'What are you doing? You weren't cleared to 2,000 feet. Go back up! Go back up! Go back up!'* The air traffic controller might let you get away with it, but if you alter your altitude by more than 500 feet, the computer takes note of the infraction automatically. So, three months later I got the letter."

Although Freeman may have had his pilot's wings clipped, it did little to dampen his high flying dreams. Next, he decided, was "Outer space. I'd like to go to the space station."

Soaring to new, previously unrivaled career heights would have to do instead.

DURING A CBS interview, Myrna Freeman was asked if her husband was a narcissist. She thought a moment. "Narcissist strikes me as somebody who's in love with themselves. I don't see him as in love with himself—he's more—*full of* himself," she laughed. "He's self-absorbed."

So does criticism bother him?

"Not that I've ever noticed."

Except when it's Morgan doing the criticizing; for someone who exudes confidence in his acting abilities, it's curious to learn that he is squeamish about watching himself on film.

"When I was doing theater, I was very successful at believing that I was great, God's gift to the theater," he explains with a laugh. "That's what they say. They come up and they say, '*You were fabulous.*' Okay, that's good, but I didn't see *The Taming of the Shrew,* and so I believe you. I want to believe you. I want to see myself through your eyes."

But he watches movies with his own eyes and says, "I see every false move." Specifically, he sees himself in the character.

"Someone was telling me that Jack Nicholson . . . said what he has to do for every role, is to work at De-Jacking, getting Jack out of the way, and you recognize that that's the truth of it. That is the task. When you read it, you can see the character and the character isn't you. The character is the character. You want to shed all of whatever is going on here and just put on that suit and wear it constantly, which is why I don't like to see myself in the movies because myself is what I see. You can feel anyway that you want, you can try and hide any way that you want, but you're not going to hide from yourself."

If he could get away with it, Freeman wouldn't go to premieres, but it would disrespectful to the others who worked on the film. "If I didn't go to see the final cut, the director would say, '*What's the matter, you're not proud of what we did?*' So, I *have* to see the final cut, but I don't like to. And no—I won't go to the dailies or watch the videotapes. I don't want to see myself."

One has to wonder what false moves he might have picked up on in *Million Dollar Baby*. The film, based on two stories in *Rope Burns*, a collection of short stories by F. X. Toole—a pseudonym for real-life ring man Jerry Boyd—tells the story of Maggie Fitzgerald, played by Hilary Swank, a wannabe fighter who convinces long-time trainer Frankie Dunn to groom her. But contrary to one snarky description, this *isn't* "Rocky in a bra."

Freeman plays one of Dunn's former boxers, Eddie "Scrap-Iron" Dupris, who lost the sight in one eye after Dunn threw in the towel one hit too late. Scrap is now Dunn's best and only friend and helps run Frankie's gym.

Even with his stellar track record as a filmmaker, Eastwood had to knock on some doors to get the film made. This wasn't a movie they were just queuing up to do," he told the *New York Times*. "I told them it's not a boxing movie. It's a love story that just happens to take place on the periphery of the boxing world—a father-daughter love story. It was turned down by a lot of people. I wasn't coming in with a .44 Magnum and doing the old genre thing. In my old age, I'm looking for things that interest me a little more."

Finally, Warner Brothers stepped up to the plate—or saying they threw their financial hat into the ring may be more apropos—putting up half the money, as did Lakeshore Entertainment. But even then, it wasn't considered a major release.

"This picture was a small picture in the scheme of things. It was all kind of loosey, and it wasn't made, like *Alexander* or *Polar Express*, with a view to how it was going to be released."

Once financing was set, he sent the script to Morgan Freeman. "That part was written for a white man," Eastwood said in a *Psychology Today* interview. "The role could have been played by a white man or a black man or a man of any race. I'd like to think that we are at the point where it is irrelevant."

It didn't take Freeman long to make a decision. "A good script is . . . not just a character, or the story or the location. It's everything. This was one of those. . . . Scripts like that don't come down the pike in large numbers, and they will go to someone other than you, if you don't move quickly. So, it's like trying to reach out and grab a fast train. I put the script down and I was ready to go on the set."

The character was so defined, Morgan says all he had to do was dress Scrap.

> The best fun you have in creating a character is in the costume department. I always like to find the hat. And then props just dress the set. It's all fabulous.
>
> It's like anything. If the writer has been successful, there's stuff that you have to do. Say the words and as [Spencer] Tracy said, "*Don't bump into the furniture.*" People hear that and say I'm being modest, but I am not a modest person, but I have to be truthful about what I'm doing and what I'm doing is channeling. I know it. I think perhaps not everybody believes it's easy and perhaps it's not easy for everybody. It's easy for me. If I find if I have to work at it, I've got the wrong job.

Freeman echoes Eastwood's characterization of *Baby* as a character study that just happens to be set in the world of fighting. "The movie isn't about boxing. It's about these people. Boxing is like a platform. It's just a stage where this is played out."

Just as he had on *Unforgiven*, Freeman found Eastwood's directorial style gave him room to fully create.

> But you better know what you're doing when you are on set because he's got his hands on the picture. His hands are not on you. And I'm one of those actors that respond very well to that.
>
> Obviously, if you're calm in your surroundings, you have a sense of security about where you are and what you're doing. Clint comes prepared. He's very prepared—he's done his homework, and you can't see it but he works hard, so . . . he's grounded and knows what he's doing. He's got great backup, people who work with him all of the time, and everybody works with him for the same reason: he expects you to your job. He's not micromanaging at all.
>
> You don't get those performances out of people. You let people do those performances.
>
> I'd like to be on a set sometime when an actor came on board and didn't know what he was doing. I'd like to hear what Clint would have to say to him. He's very helpful and forthcoming, but he usually gets good people and just stays out of the way. He sets the scene up, lights it, explains the parameters of the technical aspects, but you're not going to get direction.

Freeman agrees with director Mike Nichols, who once said, "The essence of directing is casting."

Freeman's on-screen chemistry with Swank was borne from their off-screen rapport. "Sometimes you get into a situation—with me, it's often where you've got a great dancing partner, someone who really can anticipate your every move, you can anticipate their every move, and you just flow together. That's Hilary."

Although the argument could be made that Scrap was informed by the same "gravitas" that has become one of Freeman's signature qualities, he saw it through an emotional prism. "I think in these characters, there is a level of pain of having lived through some pain and come out the other side with your philosophy in place. Scrap, for instance, he's all-accepting. He's not judgmental in terms of anybody else's situations or predicaments."

The movie premiered in December 2004 to universally glowing reviews. Because there hadn't been a big-budget promotional push prior to its release, *Million Dollar Baby* had come seemingly out of nowhere but immediately began generating Academy Award buzz for the film as well as the three actors. Few were surprised when the movie was nominated for best picture, best director, best actor, best actress, best supporting actor, and best screenplay.

Having been nominated three times before had taught Freeman not to assume and not to believe all the critics and polls that showed him to be the odds-on favorite to walk away with an Oscar. Instead, he shifted the focus onto the unprecedented number of minority nominees besides himself, including Don Cheadle and Sophie Okonedo for *Hotel Rwanda*; Catalina Sandino Marino for *Mary Full of Grace,* and Jamie Foxx, twice, for *Ray* and *Collateral.*

"What makes this year significant is the number of people of color nominated," Freeman said. "It really is a banner year. A lot of people have been down on the industry for not offering enough roles or not giving credit to the roles that are. Changes are taking place industrywide. There has been a big array of diversity. People of color are really moving into their own."

And the Academy honored Freeman as an actor in a class of his own by awarding him the best supporting Oscar. When Renée Zellweger announced his name, Freeman's peers rose in unison for a standing ovation. Morgan would later comment that "getting a standing ovation was kind of humbling that so many people are so happy that I have been named for this award. A lot of people say you're due—maybe you are, maybe you aren't—it's an accolade."

But the outpouring of respect and appreciation was "one of the things that I feel like I'm blessed with, that I'm well-thought-of, and, you know, you can take that with you throughout life if you know you're well-thought-of."

On the podium, Freeman kept his speech short. "I want to thank everybody and anybody who ever had anything to do with the making of this picture, but I especially want to thank Clint Eastwood for giving me the opportunity to work with him again and to work with Hilary Swank. This was a labor of love. And I thank the Academy. I thank you, so very much."

Prior to finally winning, Freeman admitted he had "become philosophical about the Oscars. It occurred to me that winning the nomination is probably the height of it. It is pretty much as far as you can go, and the rest of it is pretty much arbitrary . . . after you win, all of that goes out the window."

Although Freeman admitted that for as honored and humbled as he was, winning wasn't a complete shock, either, considering it a kind of career achievement nod. "I knew the next time I got nominated I was probably going to be given it. Now, I have this high profile and everybody knows me."

After winning the Oscar, Freeman continued to be Hollywood's busiest actor and continued to quietly open new doors. In *Bruce Almighty*, he played a character with the highest possible profile— God. Starring Jim Carey, the film earned over $170 million in the first three weeks of its release and provoked discussion by its portrayal of God as a black man.

"It's significant because it would not have happened twenty or thirty years ago," theologian Professor James H. Cone told the *New York Times*. "The use of a black God reflects how much white Americans can relax with the idea of racial inclusiveness, provided it doesn't challenge their power."

The fact it was Morgan Freeman didn't hurt either. Steve Oedekerk told reporter Samuel Freedman they wanted Morgan for his "combination of authority, wisdom and comic timing. We all knew having a black God was a choice that would be talked about but I don't think we were thinking it would be as groundbreaking as it turned out being. I was personally surprised by the attention this received. For me this type of casting isn't as groundbreaking as it is overdue."

While Freeman has quietly and consistently broken down barriers, when *60 Minutes* correspondent Mike Wallace asked him how to end racism, Freeman showed some heat. "Stop talking about it. I'm going to stop calling you a white man. And I'm going to ask you to stop calling me a black man. I know you as Mike Wallace. You know me as Morgan Freeman. You wouldn't say, 'Well, *I know this white guy named Mike Wallace.*' You know what I'm saying?"

He was equally outspoken about Black History Month, calling it "ridiculous. You're going to relegate my history to a month? I don't want a Black History Month. Black history is American history," pointing out there are not Caucasian or Jewish History months and saying singling out blacks fosters racism.

Although Freeman has rarely discussed politics publicly over the course of his career, he has been vocal about America's involvement in Iraq. "I'm very worried about what's going on in the world at the moment because we have this Napoleonic president—by Napoleonic I mean he's a man who just seems to need to search himself. It doesn't make sense. I don't have any love loss on Saddam Hussein. If he needs to be removed from office, fine. You have to find the right way to do it, but going to war? . . . To do what? What is the real reason?"

But, as always, he remains philosophical. "Ernest Hemingway once wrote, *The world is a fine place and worth fighting for.* I agree with the second part."

He is equally thoughtful about his own life and the creative fire that still burned in his belly. "In life, it doesn't really matter about your age. It has to do with your stride. Truly, it is it. You know, when I was in my fifties, I felt really powerful, really strong, really in good, vigorous, robust health and everything, and now I'm approaching seventy and I think I'm beginning to, like, sort of even flow."

But that doesn't mean he isn't still interested in taking on new challenges, so in July 2005, Revelations Entertainment and Intel Corporation announced the formation of a new digital entertainment company,

ClickStar Inc., to distribute first-run movies directly to consumers over the Internet

"ClickStar addresses the growing worldwide consumer demand for digital content—especially filmed entertainment," Freeman says. "Our goal is to deliver first-run premium entertainment to film fans around the world and to make film easier to buy than to pirate."

Regardless of what hat he might occasionally wear—producer, entrepreneur, sailor, pilot, cowboy—as long as the phone keeps ringing, Freeman will keep doing what he does best. "All my life . . . as far back as I can remember—I saw my first movie when I was six years old—and since then I wanted to do [act]. I wanted to be a part of that. I will always do it. I'll find a hole somewhere—a box, a barn, a stage—I'll find some place to get up and . . . fool around with other people who are as crazy as I am.

"I'm a firm believer that things happen as they should. The universe unfolds just as it's supposed to. I can say that life is good to me. Has been and is good. So I think my task is to be good to it. So how do you be good to life? You live it."

End Notes

CHAPTER 1

p. 1 "in the south . . . " (WED)
p. 2 "I don't care what you do . . . "(SPI)
p. 2 "I'm not an African . . . " (SPI)
p. 4 "Running . . . "(FG2)
p. 4 "I walked out the door . . . " (TS)
p. 4 "One of my uncles . . . " (FG2)
p. 5 "Up until my . . . " (GV)
p. 5 "The South Side . . . " (GV)
p. 6 "Living on the South Side . . . " (GV)
p. 6 "I grew up . . . " (CNN)
p. 7 "There is a connection . . . " (SB2)
p. 7 "There was a doll-like . . . " (AJ)
p. 7 "I was put on . . . " (AG)
p. 7 "I played . . . " (CJ)
p. 8 "As a teenager . . . " (FG2)
p. 8 "When a teacher tells you . . . " (HR)
p. 8 "I had two left . . . " (RC)
p. 8 "When I was a kid . . . " (TS)
p. 9 "I also wanted to . . . " (HR)
p. 9 "I didn't think a drama . . . " (GV)
p. 9 "He told me all the things . . . " (CNN)
p. 9 "Making Strafing runs . . . " (AG)
p. 10 "They had the planes . . . " (SJ)
p. 10 "That was the end . . . " (FG2)
p. 10 "I've always been a showoff . . . " (WC)
p. 10 "I'm born to do . . . " (AM)

CHAPTER 2

p. 13 "It was just serendipity . . . " (LJ)
p. 13 "I thought I'd just present myself . . . " (TS)
p. 13 "In February of 1961 . . . " (HR)

p. 14   "I knew what I wanted to do in my teens . . ." (MP)
p. 14   "I figured a school situation was the wisest thing . . . " (AG2)
p. 14   "This town almost killed me . . ." (AG)
p. 14   " . . . almost to a fault . . . " (AG)
p. 15   "I didn't think because I was flunking . . ." (WK)
p. 15   "I read Stanislavsky . . ." (SJ)
p. 15   "I was told that I was good in my dance-movement . . ." (FG)
p. 15   "We made tapes when we first . . ." (HR)
p. 16   "I got a good running start . . ." (JR)
p. 16   "I moved to New York because I was running . . ." (CAO)
p. 16   "Being born, leaving the Air Force . . ." (VM)
p. 16   "I learned to type . . . " (CAO)
p. 16   "My teacher in stage movement . . ." (WC)
p. 16   "That's where things started to happen . . ." (AG2)
p. 17   "Brecht, as you know . . ." (FFC)
p. 17   "I got my passport . . . " (AG2)
p. 17   "I remember I went to this audition . . . " (CAO)
p. 18   "was like working at McDonald's . . ." (CAO)
p. 18   "I was very good at them . . . " (CAO)
p. 19   "I remember making a decision . . . " (MP)
p. 19   "You do it because that's what you do . . . " (MP)
p. 19   " . . . because you've got to have threads . . . " (HR)
p. 20   "One night we were in Des Moines . . ." (FG)
p. 20   "It was a banner year . . . " (CAO)
p. 21   "It was . . . a training ground like no other . . . " (GE)
p. 21   "learned how to be a professional . . . " (RC)
p. 21   "He had very good speech . . . " (SJ)
p. 21   "It was a three character play . . . " (JR)
p. 21   "I was doing fine . . . " (GJ)
p. 23   "If the most important thing to happen . . . " (HL)
p. 23   "All the New York actors were going to Hollywood . . . " (JR)
p. 24   "But he was a junkie for reading . . ." (MJKO)
p. 24   "Like many people, I spoke at a higher register . . ." (CAO)
p. 24   "I could hardly stand to get up . . . " (DH)
p. 25   "He's a wonderful singer, great dancer . . . " (PB)
p. 25   "I'm not an alcoholic or anything but . . . " (SJ)
p. 25   "You start off going to lunch . . ." (HR)
p. 25   "My marriage was breaking up . . ." (QT)
p. 25   "I'd bought a boat in 1967 . . . " (RC)
p. 26   "One of my nightmares . . ." (WC)
p. 26   "I've seen reruns of it once or twice . . . " (SB4)
p. 26   "It should've stayed where it was . . . " (CAO)
p. 27   "Zeke is one of those guys . . . " (CJ2)
p. 27   "I thought I was ready . . . " (HR)
p. 27   "the noise was all around me . . . " (CAO)
p. 27   "I got a call, September of 1978 . . . " (FFC)

CHAPTER 3

p. 31 "Acting the part of someone who's incarcerated . . ." (HB)

p. 32 "You learn it's not what you want to do . . ." (UPI2)

p. 32 "He was very aloof, alone . . ." (TS)

p. 32 "I was hysterical to have a baby . . ." (TS)

p. 35 "I believe it was a situation . . ." (HM)

p. 35 "After Williams was jailed, the killings continued . . ." (HM)

p. 35 "When you live in the world of make-believe . . ." (SJ)

p. 35 "I used to feel best when I was acting . . ." (HR)

p. 36 "I like to live on the edge . . ." (AJ)

p. 36 "I had no intention of wearing crushed-velvet . . ." (SJ)

p. 37 "I'm frequently offered a lot of money to kill . . ." (VGL)

p. 37 "A block away from where . . ." (SB4)

p. 37 "He was a procurer . . ." (CJ2)

p. 38 "I grew up on the stage . . ." (JR)

p. 38 "On one take, he drew blood . . ." (TS)

p. 39 "I read somewhere . . ." (MM)

p. 39 "It seems to me that I never grow . . ." (FG)

p. 39 "It's kind of hard to explain . . ." (MM)

p. 39 "Because when I look at it, I see a side . . ." (JR)

p. 39 "It's always great when someone sings . . ." (CAO)

p. 39 "change anything. It only changes . . ." (MM)

p. 39 "it was an excellent thing to read . . ." (SPI)

p. 40 "Bad guys are complex . . ." (TJ2)

p. 40 "Chris' life was governed . . ." (FFC)

p. 41 "I was known in New York . . ." (BL)

p. 42 "I think there was a change of consciousness . . ." (FG)

p. 42 "I was comfortable in front of a camera . . ." (AG)

CHAPTER 4

p. 45 "flocked backstage, bawling . . ." (DH)

p. 46 "You talk about great timing . . ." (WC)

p. 46 "Every tenth year of my life . . ." (CAO)

p. 46 "The press come around and tell you . . ." (DH)

p. 47 "Everything that's done for television . . ." (HR)

p. 47 "I really don't want to get stuck . . ." (MV)

p. 48 "I enjoyed that experience . . ." (JR)

p. 49 "I discovered cocaine . . ." (TS)

p. 49 "I had to go through that . . ." (HA)

p. 49 "many of them were based . . ." (HR)

p. 50 "You're a bit young . . ." (DH)

p. 51 "It started out as an odd . . ." (HR)

p. 53 "I spent a lot of time with Joe . . ." (SS2)

p. 54 "In movies, you have to simplify . . ." (CJ2)

p. 55 "Getting jobs is only a problem . . ." (VM)

p. 55 "You go to movies and it's science fiction . . ." (HR)
p. 55 "That instant gratification . . ." (SS2)

CHAPTER 5

p. 58 "I didn't know anybody who acted like that . . ." (HL)
p. 58 "And so we put this movie together . . ." (JR)
p. 58 "I have a special affinity . . ." (WC)
p. 59 "I read history as a hobby . . ." (MV)
p. 59 "You go along, and you work . . ." (BJ)
p. 59 "It's one of the most important things . . ." (DH)
p. 59 "*Glory* . . . had something to teach . . ." (DR)
p. 60 "I studied slave narratives . . ." (CJ2)
p. 61 "This is the kind of picture . . ." (CG)
p. 62 "I was a city girl . . ." (AJ)
p. 62 "I was shaped and molded by the South . . ." (GV)
p. 62 "I swore I'd never come back to live . . ." (PJ)
p. 62 "Growing up in Mississippi . . ." (FG)
p. 63 "It's a certain attitude about life and other people . . ." (BJ)
p. 63 "When I moved home, all my neighbors . . ." (BL)

CHAPTER 6

p. 65 "My understanding of acting is that it's pretending . . ." (DR)
p. 66 "Everywhere we went, we heard . . ." (CP2)
p. 67 "I think Morgan could do . . ." (DH)
p. 67 "It turned me off . . ." (SB4)
p. 67 "The thing about Hoke . . ." (CJ2)
p. 68 "My father worked as a domestic . . ." (FM)
p. 68 "People who don't know the South . . ." (CAO)
p. 73 "Boy, you've gotta be careful . . ." (SB3)
p. 73 "I always explain my life . . ." (WC)
p. 73 "But you can't take . . ." (SB3)
p. 73 "a deep and abiding sense of humor . . ." (TS)
p. 75 "It was the first time that I froze . . ." (FFC)
p. 75 "I was on the stage a long time . . ." (MM)
p. 76 "will choose me. There's a lot . . ." (WC)

CHAPTER 7

p. 77 "You're not really successful . . ." (RE)
p. 78 "I don't particularly care . . ." (WC)
p. 78 "I try always to go beyond the image . . ." (PB)
p. 78 "Driving Miss Daisy kind of ruined . . ." (APW)
p. 80 "Originally they hired Alan Arkin . . ." (SB4)
p. 81 "One critic said of Robin Hood . . ." (FG)

p. 82 "The thing I remember most is being in pain . . . " (SB4)

p. 84 "a childhood dream come true . . . " (GJ)

p. 84 "Until I was 15 years old . . . " (AM)

p. 84 "One of my favorite movies . . . " (CAO)

p. 85 "I was in Africa . . . " (FFC)

p. 85 "That would have been apologetic . . . " (FG)

p. 85 "I'd never seen him in person . . . " (MWO)

p. 85 "What I like most about Clint . . . " (CAO)

CHAPTER 8

p. 90 "I'd been looking at the idea kind of sideways . . . " (RD)

p. 90 "I grew up going to movies . . . " (GJ)

p. 90 "I'd seen that done . . . " (BL2)

p. 90 "Micah believes . . . " (EW)

p. 91 "The world is made up . . . " (GJ)

p. 91 "The story could have been set . . . " (RD)

p. 91 "A man does the best he can for himself . . . " (ATC)

p. 92 "We had to be careful that this family . . . " (HJ)

p. 92 "policemen's wives, all ex-wives . . . " (FFC)

p. 93 "It's tough to see people who cannot . . . " (EW)

p. 93 "Coming there to make a movie . . . " (BL2)

p. 93 "As soon as I got inside . . . " (EW)

p. 93 "is a luxury for a movie . . . " (RD)

p. 94 "third eye. When you're on stage . . . " (EW)

p. 94 "I think having control is having kid gloves . . . " (GJ)

p. 94 "As you go through working with people . . . " (ATC)

p. 94 "You spend a lot of time saying . . . " (BL2)

p. 95 "is the epitome of how . . . " (HJ)

p. 95 "I think sometimes you throw the dice . . . " (BL2)

p. 95 "The entertainment industry does not operate . . . " (GJ)

p. 95 "I want them to say . . . " (BL2)

p. 96 "I think the story is about accepting . . . " (RD)

p. 98 "It was a great experience . . . " (MV)

p. 98 "I'm spoiled by working in a movie . . . " (JLW)

p. 98 "He'll disappear in the morning . . . " (AJ)

p. 98 "Having traveled around the country . . . " (FP)

p. 99 "You can exist down there . . . " (CAO)

CHAPTER 9

p. 102 "I never ask that . . . " (HC)

p. 102 "It's a love affair . . . " (HB)

p. 102 "I think that's what resonates . . . " (DR)

p. 102 "You never actually knew . . . " (TJ2)

p. 103 "For me, someone who comes . . . " (HB)

p. 104 "They ran a whole bunch of . . . " (JR)
p. 104 "Tim and I, we work in the same way . . . " (HB)
p. 104 "I have a problem with writer-directors . . . " (JR)
p. 105 "I think the appeal is there . . . " (FP)
p. 105 "Everywhere I go, everywhere I go . . . " (JR)
p. 107 "I think I've been pigeonholed . . . " (DR)
p. 107 "I'm concerned about being bracketed . . . " (KE)
p. 107 "I don't get any chance to do humor . . . " (TJ2)
p. 107 "any favors at all, it has been rejecting . . . (DR)
p. 107 "I'm good at nasty." (BL)
p. 108 "It occurred to me that winning the nomination . . . " (BBC)

CHAPTER 10

p. 110 "I'm the older guy, the thinker . . . " (MM2)
p. 110 "very, very immediate to me . . . " (JR)
p. 111 "delightful; one of those people . . . " (MV)
p. 111 "That's rumor . . . " (JR)
p. 111 "He's a professional . . . " (MV)
p. 111 "He is very computer literate . . . " (JR)
p. 112 "I seldom get into the mood . . . " (FG)
p. 114 "There's all this loss and angst . . . " (SB4)
p. 114 "I don't want the audience to get a message . . . " (PW)
p. 114 "The press were in my face . . . " (SS)
p. 115 "It's natural evolution . . . " (BG)
p. 116 "I told my daughter . . . " (KC)
p. 117 "It's incumbent upon us . . . " (MM2)

CHAPTER 11

p. 119 "He is an extremely wealthy individual . . . " (J2)
p. 120 "Everyone I've talked to . . . " (JLW)
p. 120 "A project has to hit us in the gut . . . " (RJ)
p. 120 "The idea was to make movies . . . " (TB)
p. 120 "I figured the way to get it done is . . . " (SS)
p. 120 "Like *Bopha!*, some of these movies . . . " (RJ)
p. 121 "When I was doing press for *Deep Impact* . . . " (SB4)
p. 121 "If you're just pretending, they can handle it . . . " (WB)
p. 121 "I am going to stop here a moment . . . " (JR)
p. 122 "I developed a philosophy over the years . . . " (WB)
p. 122 "When you're hot . . . " (RJ)
p. 122 "The reality of life is that tomorrow . . . " (WB)
p. 122 "I enjoy sailing . . . " (CJ3)
p. 123 "and I remember watching this other dancer . . . " (MB)
p. 123 "I can remember times . . . " (CJ3)
p. 123 "What governs us . . . " (LJW)

p. 123 "When you're young, you dream . . . " (MB)
p. 123 "I have all the toys I ever wanted . . . " (WB)
p. 124 "I think Christian . . . " (QT)
p. 124 "I often think I am probably quite lucky . . . " (TJ2)
p. 124 "The film was originally called *The Flood* . . . " (TM3)
p. 125 "It's a weird thing, a strange dichotomy . . . " (FFC)
p. 125 "I have to reconcile myself to the saintliness . . . " (DR3)
p. 126 "It's all about working . . . " (BJ)
p. 126 "They contacted me about the honor . . . " (RJ)
p. 126 "I think I'm enough of a technician . . . " (SPI)
p. 127 "You can be rejuvenated . . . " (TJ2)
p. 127 "You may absolutely assume . . . " (CJ3)
p. 127 "When I think of things like *Glory* . . . " (TB)
p. 127 "I was drawn mostly to the picture itself . . . " (TJ2)
p. 129 "Another one of those moments . . . " (JR)
p. 129 "Steven calls up . . . " (LAS)
p. 129 "Here were people who were kidnapped . . . " (TJ2)
p. 129 "Number one I can't believe the luck . . . " (JR)
p. 129 "Actually, that's a two-edged sword . . . " (EW)
p. 129 "But on something like *Amistad* . . . " (RE)
p. 129 "He's exciting . . . " (JR)
p. 130 "You know, I have had two really outstanding . . . " (CJ3)
p. 131 "is subject matter that Americans . . . " (SB4)
p. 131 "The only color in that town is green . . . " (QT)
p. 131 "I loved the film . . . " (JR)
p. 132 "Let me just say this . . . " (BJ)
p. 132 "The whole thing was that eventually . . . " (FFC)
p. 132 "I really do like making movies . . . " (CJ3)

CHAPTER 12

p. 133 "If they say that to me and it's true . . . " (JR)
p. 133 "The man in *Se7en* was old . . . " (SB)
p. 133 "What's the background of the average . . . " (SJ)
p. 134 "Acting is merely an interpretive . . . " (SPI)
p. 136 "I don't keep in touch . . . " (SB2)
p. 136 "Her sense of humor . . . " (SB2)
p. 136 "Gary Fleder is a young man . . . " (JR)
p. 138 "You get some roles because you're Black . . . " (MP)
p. 138 "This is where we are . . . " (SB3)
p. 138 "If you want studio power . . . " (MP)
p. 139 "very excited, because what I thought . . . " (MJO)
p. 139 "I think that the great unsung heroes . . . " (JR)
p. 139 "Working with Gene Hackman was the main . . . " (KE)
p. 140 "Wherever he goes with what he does . . . " (JR)
p. 140 "This was a very intense piece . . . " (SB3)

p. 140 "Between shots, yeah, I just chill . . . " (KE)
p. 141 "I'm a joyous worker . . . " (SB3)
p. 141 "You can say to me . . . " (JR)
p. 141 "Normally, if you're doing a film . . . " (MJO)
p. 141 "Because Under Suspicion is essentially . . . " (JR)
p. 143 "It happens to all of us." (EC)

CHAPTER 13

p. 147 "I knew there was a massive . . . " (SF)
p. 147 "This country was built by an awfully . . . " (WW)
p. 147 "I know that I am informed about history . . . " (JR)
p. 147 "tells of moments in American history . . . " (SF)
p. 147 "Since the Emancipation Proclamation . . . " (MB)
p. 147 "What criteria are you going to use . . . " (WW)
p. 148 "These men stood up for their rights . . . " (MB)
p. 149 "There's a real human element to the story . . . " (SF)
p. 149 "It's now history, and time . . . " (WW)
p. 149 "On the one hand, I don't think . . . " (UPI)
p. 149 "I'm drawn to these things . . . " (KE)
p. 150 "The only thing that attracts me about any group . . . " (SB3)
p. 150 "I was on hiatus . . . " (MB)
p. 150 "This is one of those cases when you say . . . " (SB3)
p. 150 "I saw his first movie, In the Company of Men . . . " (SB4)

CHAPTER 14

p. 153 "You might imagine that I got paid . . . " (LJW)
p. 153 "Alex is not my favorite role . . . " (VM)
p. 154 "We're always seeing places . . . " (MWO2)
p. 155 "It keeps us both grounded . . . " (JLW)
p. 155 "Those were my parents . . . " (AJ)
p. 155 "Once you get something like this started . . . " (JLW)
p. 155 "One reason to be back here . . . " (SA)
p. 156 "You could have built a forty-story . . . " (AJ)
p. 156 "Bill has renovated numerous . . . " (JLW)
p. 157 "You have the devil . . . " (ER)
p. 157 "I think it behoove us . . . " (WW)
p. 157 "We were always hearing on the street . . . " (SA)
p. 158 "Clarksdale is the crossroads . . . " (JLW)
p. 158 "What we have to give thanks for . . . " (GE)
p. 158 "Sometimes when I am home . . . " (SA)
p. 159 "The flag, the stars and bars . . . " (CW)
p. 159 "That flag and the KKK . . . " (AJ)
p. 159 "I know that the bulk of the people . . . " (ZWO)
p. 160 "They still feel that they do not have a say . . . " (CNN)
p. 160 "Morgan felt slapped . . . " (AJ)

CHAPTER 15

CHAPTER 16

Works Cited

Adderton, Donald. *Delta Democrat Times*, March 30, 2001. (AD)

All Things Considered (NPR), September 25, 1993. (ALC)

Anderson, Matt. MovieHabit.com http://www.moviehabit.com/essays/ freeman04.shtml. (AM)

AP Online, February 10, 2003. (APO)

AP Worldstream, September 2, 2005. (APW)

Arnold, Gary. *The Washington Times*, October 31, 1997. (AG)

Arnold, Gary. *The Washington Times*, May 31, 2002. (AG2)

Ascher-Walsh, Rebecca. *Entertainment Weekly*, August 16, 1996. (AWR)

Auchmutey, Jim. *The Atlanta Journal and Constitution*, July 1, 2001. (AJ)

————. *The Palm Beach Post*, August 12, 2001. (AJ2)

Baird, Lisa G. *The Record* (Bergen County, NJ), September 26, 1993. (BL2)

Barboza, Craigh. *Daily News*, from the *New York Times*, November 4, 1996. (BG)

Beale, Lewis. *Newsday*, June 1, 2005. (BL)

Beckerman, Jim. *The Record* (Bergen County, NJ), October 1, 1997. (BJ)

Berkman, Meredith. *Entertainment Weekly*, October 22, 1993. (BM)

Bourne, Kay. *Bay State Banner*, October 17, 1996. (BK)

Breznican, Anthony. *AP Worldstream*, March 21, 2003. (BA)

Carr, Jay. *Boston Globe*, January 12, 1990. (CJ)

————. *Boston Globe*, January 7, 1990. (CJ2)

————. *Boston Globe*, December 7, 1997. (CJ3)

Cawthorne, Alec. BBC.com; http://www.bbc.co.uk/films/2002/10/08/ morgan_freeman_high_crimes_interview.shtml. (CA)

CBSnews.com, January 27, 2005. http://www.cbsnews.com/stories/2005/01/26/ earlyshow/leisure/celebspot/main669552.shtml. (CBS)

Celebritywonder.com. http://www.celebritywonder.com/html/ morganfreeman_bio1.html. (CW)

Chung, Philip W. *AsianWeek*, March 23, 2005. (CP)

Chutkow, Paul. *New York Times*, April 8, 1990. (CP2)

CNN; People in the News; http://edition.cnn.com/TRANSCRIPTS/0208/17/ pitn.00.html. (CNN)

Coe, Richard L. *The Washington Post*, March 8, 1978. (CR)

Collins, Glenn. *New York Times*, March 26, 1989. (CG)

Crowther, Bosley. *New York Times*, August 4, 1966. (CB)

Cunningham, Kim. *People Weekly*, October 10, 1994. (CK)

———. *People Weekly*, May 17, 1993. (CK2)

———. *People Weekly*, August 23, 1993. (CK3)

Daily Record (Glasgow, Scotland). February 19, 2003. (DR)

Daily Variety. February 28, 2005. (DV)

Dawidziak, Mark. *The News & Record*, March 6, 1996. (DM)

Denerstein, Robert. *Rocky Mountain News*, October 23, 2004. (DR2)

Driscoll, Rob. *Western Mail* (Cardiff, Wales), August 17, 2002. (DR3)

Dudar, Helen. *New York Times*, December 10, 1989. (DH)

Ealy, Charles. *The Dallas Morning News*, October 13, 2000. (EC)

Elder, Robert. *Chicago Tribune*, April 7, 2001. (ER)

Ellison II, Willie. *Precinct Reporter*, September 30, 1993. (EW)

Filmfreakcentral.com; http://www.filmfreakcentral.net/notes/
mfreemaninterview.htm. (FFC)

Fischer, Paul. FilmMonthly.com. http://www.filmmonthly.com/Profiles/Articles/
MFreeman/MFreeman.html. (FP)

Fors, Myra. *New York Times*, June 4, 1989. (FM)

Freedman, Samuel G. *New York Times*, June 11, 2003. (FG)

Fuller, Graham. Interview, June 1, 1996. (FG2)

Garner, Jack. Gannett News Service, May 28, 2002. (GJ)

Gerstel, Judy. Knight Ridder/Tribune News Service, September 23, 1993. (GJ2)

Givens, Robin. *Ebony*, June 1, 1991. (GR)

Golphin, Vincent F.A. *about . . . time Magazine*, February 28, 1995. (GV)

Gordon, Ed. NPR Special, May 13, 2005. (GE)

Groves, Bob. *The Record* (Bergen County, NJ), August 7, 1992. (GB)

Hall, Allan. *The Mirror*, January 4, 1996. (HA)

Harrington, Richard. The Washington Post, March 3, 1989. (HR)

Hartl, John. The Seattle Times, January 17, 1988. (HJ)

Hewitt, Chris. Knight Ridder/Tribune News Service, May 28, 2002. (HC)

Hill, Michael. *The Washington Post*, February 10, 1985. (HM)

Holsey, Steve. *Michigan Chronicle*, March, 8 2005. (HS)

Hood-Adams, Rebecca. *Clarksdale Press Register*, http://www.zwire.com/site/news.
cfm?newsid=2400596&BRD=2038&PAG=461&dept_id=230613&rfi=8. (HAR)

———. *Clarksdale Press Register*, http://www.zwire.com/site/
news.cfm?newsid=1873211&BRD=2038&PAG=461&dept_id=230613&rfi=8.
(HAR2)

Horne, Lena. *Ebony*, November 1, 1990. (HL)

Hruska, Bronwen. *Entertainment Weekly*, September 30, 1994 (HB)

http://www.celebritywonder.com/html/morganfreeman_bio1.html. (CWO)

http://www.cigaraficionado.com/Cigar/CA_Profiles/People_Profile/
0,2540,207,00.html. (CAO)

http://www.contactmusic.com/new/home.nsf/webpages/morganx06x08x02. (CMO)

http://getaway.ninemsn.com.au/article.aspx?ID=54058 June 29, 2005. (GAO)

http://www.indielondon.co.uk/film/batman_begins_freeman.html. (ILO)

http://www.truthout.org/docs_05/011805Z.shtml. (TOO)

http://www.zwire.com/site/news.cfm?newsid=1635543&BRD=2038&PAG=
461&dept_id=230613&rfi=8. (ZWO)

Hubbard, Kim. *People Weekly*, August 6, 1990. (HK)

Huver, Scott. Hollywood.com; http://www.hollywood.com/movies/feature/id/2441516. (HS2)

Ign.com, Jeff Otto IGN.com; http://filmforce.ign.com/articles/572/572407p1.html. (IJO)

Jet. October 17, 1994. (J)

Jet. August 12, 1996. (J2)

Jet. July 4, 2005. (J3)

Jeter, Lynne Wilbanks. *Mississippi Magazine*, January 1, 2002. (JLW)

Jobson, Richard. FilmGuardian.com http://film.guardian.co.uk/interview/interviewpages/0,6737,344698,00.html. (JR)

Jones, Alison. *The Birmingham Post* (England), August 19, 2002. (JA)

Kaufman, David. *New York Times*, August 2, 1987. (KD)

Kennedy, Lisa. *The Denver Post*, October 25, 2004. (KL)

Kim, Ellen A. Hollywood.com, September 18, 2000. http://www.hollywood.com/features/t1/nav/5/id/473420. (KE)

Kim, Ellen A. Hollywood.com, http://www.hollywood.com/features/t1/nav/5/id/470359. (KE2)

Kinnon, Joy Bennett. *Ebony*, January 1997. (KJB)

Kopp, Craig. *The Cincinnati Post*, June 13, 1996. (KC)

Lancaster, Jordan. University Wire, March 28, 2003. (JL)

Lentz, Philip. *Chicago Tribune*, March 26, 1989. (LP)

LJWorld.com. http://www2.ljworld.com/news/2001/apr/05/nailed_to_the/. (LJW)

Los Angeles Sentinel. March 26, 1997. (LAS)

Lovell, Glenn. Knight Ridder/Tribune News Service, September 22, 1994. (LG)

Lyman, Rick. *New York Times*, February 27, 2002. (LR)

Macdonald, Moira. Knight Ridder/Tribune News Service; March 28, 2002. (MM)

Millard, Rosie. *New Statesman*, May 5, 2003. (MR)

Miller, Prairie. *Star Interviews*, January 1, 2000. (MP)

Mills, Bart. *Chicago Tribune*, March 28, 1999. (MB)

Mixon, Veronica. *Philadelphia Tribune*, September 15, 1995. (MV)

Moore, Marie. *New York Beacon*, October 4, 1995. (MM2)

Morales, Wilson. Blackfilm.com; http://www.blackfilm.com/20041210/features/morganfreeman.shtml. (MWO)

———. Blackfilm.com, http://www.blackfilm.com/20050520/features/morganfreeman.shtml. (MWO2)

Moses, Gavin. *People Weekly*, March 27, 1989. (MG)

Mottram, James. http://www.bbc.co.uk/films/2001/01/11/morgan_freeman_under_suspicion_090101_interview.shtml (MJO)

M2 Presswire, July 6, 2005. (M2P)

Muir, John Kenneth. http://www.johnkennethmuir.com/JohnKennethMuirsRetroTVFile_TheElectricCompany.html. (MJKO)

Muller, Bill. *The Arizona Republic*, May 26, 2002. (MB2)

Murray, Rebecca Murray and Fred Topel. http://movies.about.com/library/weekly/aalevityintc.htm. (MRM)

Owens, David. *Clarksdale Press Register*, February 26, 2005. (OD)

People Weekly. October 16, 1995. (PW)

Pinsker, Beth. *The Dallas Morning News*, June 9, 1996. (PB)

Pitt, Will. January 17, 2005; http://www.cinecon.com/news.php?id=0506142. (PW)

Prescott, Jean. Knight Ridder/Tribune News Service, August 21, 2001. (PJ)

Psychology Today. January–February 1993; http://www.psychologytoday.com/
    articles/pto-19930101-000019.html (PTO)

Quinn, Thomas. *The Mirror* (London, England), March 5, 1998. (QT)

Rickey, Carrie. Knight Ridder/Tribune News Service, April 30, 2001. (RC)

Ringel, Eleanor. *Atlanta Journal and Constitution*, December 10, 1997. (RE)

Roberts, Jerry. *Variety*, September 1, 1997. (RJ)

Roberts, Kimberly C. *Philadelphia Tribune*, February 25, 2005. (RK)

Robertson, Nan. *New York Times*, May 25, 1987. (RN)

Ryan, Desmond. Knight Ridder/Tribune News Service, October 6, 1993. (RD)

Sachs, Andrea. *The Washington Post*, November 13, 2005. (SA)

Schaefer, Stephen. *The Boston Herald*, October 2, 1997. (SS)

Seattle Post-Intelligencer. October 15, 1997. (SPI)

Shuster, Fred. *Daily News*, March 24, 1999. (SF)

Simpson, Janice C. *Time*, January 8, 1990. (SJ)

Smith, Sid. *Chicago Tribune*, March 5, 1989. (SS2)

Stoner, Patrick. http://www.whyy.org/flicks/Freeman_Kiss_interview.html. (SPO)

Strauss, Bob. Daily News; October 1, 1997. (SB)

———. *Daily News*, March 5, 2002. (SB2)

———. *Daily News*, September 24, 2000. (SB3)

Strickler, Jeff. *Minneapolis Star-Tribune*, September 28, 1997. (SJ2)

Svetkey, Benjamin. *Entertainment Weekly*, March 20, 2001. (SB4)

The Mirror (London, England). April 24, 1998. (TM)

The Mirror. August 18, 2003. (TM2)

The Mirror. April 24, 1998. (TM3)

Thomas, Bob. AP Online, March 27, 1999. (TB)

Toepfer, Susan. *People Weekly*, April 4, 1988. (TS)

Trescott, Jacqueline. *The Washington Post*, February 24, 1978. (TJ)

———. *The Washington Post*, December 10, 1997. (TJ2)

United Press International. February 3, 2004. (UPI)

United Press International. April 17, 2001. (UPI2)

United Press International. February 6, 2004. (UPI3)

Van Gelder, Lawrence. *New York Times*, July 4, 1986. (VGL)

Vincent, Mal. *The Virginian Pilot*, April 6, 2001. (VM)

Waxman, Sharon. *The Washington Post*, February 16, 1999. (WS)

Wexler, Barbara. *Video Business*, September 14, 1998. (WB)

Whitaker, Charles. *Ebony*, April 1, 1990. (WC)

Williams, Edwina Dakin. *Remember Me to Tom*. 1963. (WED)

Williams, Kam. *Baltimore Afro-American*, January 28, 2005. (WK)

Williams, Wendy J. *The Boston Herald*, March 26, 1999. (WW)

Zap2It.com. September 29, 2003. (Z2I)

Films by Morgan Freeman include:

Batman Begins
War of the Worlds
Million Dollar Baby
The Sum of All Fears
Along Came a Spider
Deep Impact
Amistad
Kiss the Girls
Moll Flanders
Se7en
Outbreak
The Shawshank Redemption
Robin Hood: Prince of Thieves
Glory
Driving Miss Daisy
Lean on Me
Street Smart
Death of a Prophet
Roll of Thunder, Hear My Cry